A TREASURY OF
MENNONITE QUILTS

Lone Star

82 x 82

Cotton

circa 1915

Lancaster County, Pennsylvania

Quiltmaker: Barbara Bollinger

Owner: R. Clair Sauder

Barbara and her mother, Kate Brubaker Bollinger, made this quilt prior to Barbara's marriage to Evan Stauffer. The quilt's sawtooth border was accurately planned and executed. Each star point is sharp and precise. The border quilting is an unusual combination of a feather pattern and diagonal lines. The interior quilting delightfully blends feather wreaths, clamshell and crosshatch motifs.

The quilt was stored for most of its lifetime in chests and was used only occasionally on a spare bed. Barbara's daughter inherited the quilt, then passed it on to her son when she and her husband moved to smaller quarters to retire.

A TREASURY OF
MENNONITE QUILTS

RACHEL AND KENNETH PELLMAN

Good Books®

Intercourse, Pennsylvania 17534

Acknowledgements

We wish to thank the scores of people who have helped to make this project possible. Without the willingness of people to trust us with their irreplaceable heirlooms for controlled photography, without their trust in us to tell the stories of their quilts faithfully, this book would be only a dream.

We share your love for your quilts. Keep them in your families. Pass along a treasure and a memory.

All quilt photography by Jonathan Charles. Historical photographs were provided by the quilt owners.

Cover design by Cheryl Benner
Design by Dawn J. Ranck

A TREASURY OF MENNONITE QUILTS
© 1992 by Good Books, Intercourse, PA 17534
International Standard Book Number: 1-56148-059-2
Library of Congress Catalog Card Number: 92-26505

Library of Congress Cataloging-in-Publication Data

Pellman, Rachel T. (Rachel Thomas)
   A treasury of Mennonite quilts / Rachel and Kenneth Pellman.
      p. cm.
   Includes index.
   ISBN 1-56148-059-2 : $19.95 (deluxe pbk.)
   1. Quilts, Mennonite. I. Pellman, Kenneth, 1952- . II. Title.
NK9112.P4433 1992
746.9'7'088287--dc20

92-26505
CIP

Table of Contents

Log Cabin
86 x 88
Cotton
circa 1920
Lancaster County, Pennsylvania
Quiltmaker: Katie Funk
Owners: Richard and Betty
       Neff Pellman

Because she was a friend and was distantly related to the older woman, Betty Neff was promised one of Mrs. Katie Funk's quilts. She was a young girl when she and her only sister went to Mrs. Funk's house to each choose one of the several quilts shown to them. Betty, being the younger of the two, got second choice. She was undecided until her mother suggested this colorful Log Cabin. Betty's initials, " B.N.," were embroidered on the back before it was given to her. In this case, the initials indicate the quilt's owner, not its maker.

Introduction

This book offers a sampling of quilts made by Mennonites across North America between the late nineteenth and early twentieth centuries. The quilts shown here represent, in broad strokes, the geographical spread of Mennonites at that time.

We have defined a Mennonite quilt as one which was made by a member of a Mennonite group. In contrast to Amish quilts of the same period, which are easily identified by their use of only solid colored fabric and bold geometric shapes, Mennonite quilts use a wider variety of fabrics, patterns, and styles, which makes it difficult to establish a quilt as "Mennonite" without knowing its provenance.

All of the quilts shown here can be traced to their families of origin. While many of them are still in the hands of the quiltmakers' direct descendants, few are in the communities where they were made. As Mennonites migrated to new places because of marriage, jobs, educational pursuits and other interests, their quilts have gone with them.

The quilts shown in this book are not representative of the majority of quilts made by Mennonite women of that period. Many of the ones included here were made to commemorate a special time or occasion, and thus were lavished with care and attention to detail. They were used only on spare beds or were kept in chests and brought out to adorn beds only when company came. This kind of care preserved them well and explains their healthy condition.

Countless other quilts were also lovingly made, but were used until threadbare. Quilts were, after all, made with function as their first priority; aesthetic concerns were secondary. Despite that, a love of beauty and attention to design are clearly evident in these fabric creations. These are more than blankets to warm sleeping bodies. The makers of these quilts used quilting as an avenue for individual creative expression.

Quilting also played a role in the social fabric of the community. Church sewing circles made quilts to give as appreciation gifts to pastors and to other members of their congregations who moved away. Quilts were also made and sold as fund raisers for Mennonite relief agencies who assisted the needy around the world. Women's groups met together to quilt and, in that time, visited *and* reinforced the values of Mennonite life and thought.

Mennonites have changed over the years. They are, at the end of the twentieth century, less homogeneous, spreading from farms to cities, living on every continent, and representing many different cultures and traditions. Quilting, though still practiced actively or in the recent memory of many North American Mennonites, is no longer a cultural tradition for the majority of today's Mennonites.

Quilting, however, remains a precious legacy—both the process of creation and the end result. May this exploration of a traditional treasure open all of us to the precious symbols of other cultures and traditions.

—Rachel and Kenneth Pellman

Crazy
68 x 84
Cotton, wool
1920
Wayne County, Ohio
Quiltmaker: Hilda Mae (Gerber)
*   Lehman*
Owner: Hilda Lehman

Hilda Mae Gerber spent the summer of 1920 helping her sister Susan. Susan and her husband lived on a large farm and were adding a piece to the barn that summer. Hilda was hired to do housework and lawn and garden chores. It happened that her boyfriend, David Lehman, worked that summer at the same farm. Though they spent their days at the same location, they seldom worked together. He spent most of his time doing field work, and her assignments were largely domestic.

During her spare moments, Hilda decided to make a quilt. She arranged most of the blocks in crazy patches and outlined each of their seams with beautiful embroidery stitches. She does not remember having been taught to do the stitchery—it was something she worked out on her own.

Nine of the quilt's 30 patches break the crazy patch format. On these blocks (which are squares tipped on an angle) she carefully stitched her parents' names and birthdates and the names and birthdates of each of her siblings.

Hilda explains that when she and her brothers and sisters were born, each was given only a first name. One day, some years later, her parents called them into the living room and assigned each of them a middle name. Their "new" middle names were included on Hilda's quilt.

Hilda finished piecing the top during the summer of 1920 and, upon her return home, she gave the top to her parents. No special occasion called for such a gift. She seemed simply to want to express gratefulness to her parents. That winter she and her mother put the quilt into a frame and knotted it. Her mother thought the top would be more pleasing without knots, so they put the quilt in the frame topside down and tied the red and green knots on the back.

Hilda married David J. Lehman the following June on David's twenty-first birthday. They spent the first two years of their marriage living with Hilda's parents. Hilda helped her mother at home and David spent the summers with the thrashers. Throughout the winters he worked with a local man, butchering and peddling meat, helped on the farm and did whatever jobs were available. After two years he and Hilda rented a farm, and then eventually were able to buy their own farm. They lived together for 67 years before David died.

Hilda continued to make quilts. She made one for each of her children—two boys and two girls—prior to their marriages and has made quilts for each of her 14 grandchildren.

Quiltmaker Hilda Gerber Lehman is shown above. She made the quilt for her parents, Jacob M. and Lina A. Gerber. The Gerber homestead in Wayne County, Ohio, is shown on left.

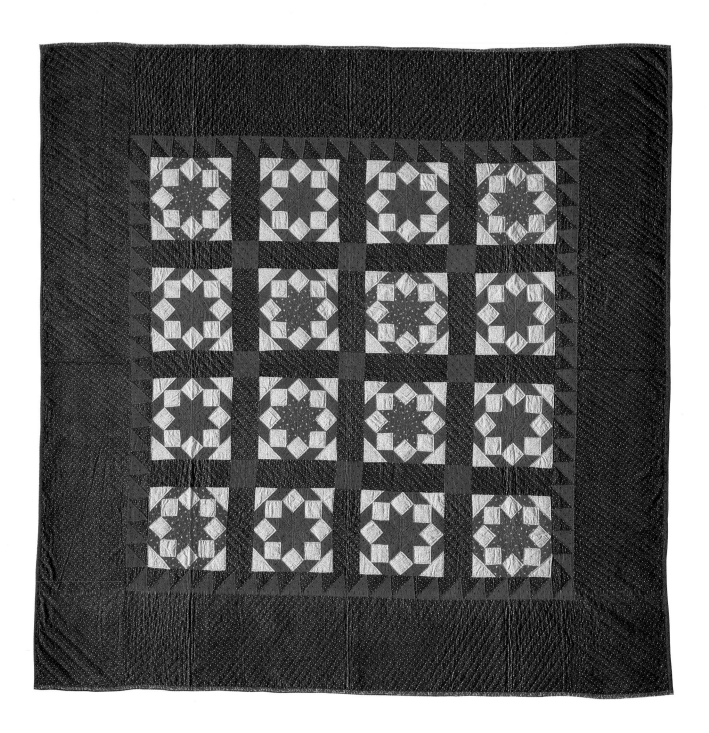

Pieced Star
85 x 85
Cotton
circa 1915
Berks County, Pennsylvania
Quiltmaker: Elizabeth Musser Weber
Owner: Mary W. Gehman

Elizabeth (Musser) Weber was the mother of 10 children—eight sons and two daughters—and the grandmother of more than 50. Elizabeth set out to make a quilt for each grandchild. Unfortunately, she died before fully completing that goal.

When her husband died in 1925, Elizabeth sold their possessions at public auction. This quilt was purchased by their daughter and given to her daughter Mary, Elizabeth's youngest grandchild, so that she, too, would have one of her grandmother's quilts.

Elizabeth Rufenacht's parents came to Wayne County, Ohio, from Switzerland in 1829. Eight years later they moved to Fulton County, a distance of about 150 miles. They were quite poor, and having no horses, each parent pulled a cart carrying their children and possessions. Elizabeth, the second child, was three years old at the time. An Amish man, seeing their need, gave them a horse. The Rufenachts were members of the Reformed church in Switzerland. It is thought that the kindness shown them by the Amish influenced them to become members of the Amish-Mennonite church.

Elizabeth made this quilt *(left)* in 1858 at the age of 24. Her initials and the date are embroidered in small letters on the top border. Elizabeth never married. She and her sister and brother lived together until their deaths. This quilt was given to a nephew, Elias Rufenacht, after her death. Elias has since passed it to his son, Reo Rufenacht.

The use of brightly colored cotton sateen fabrics make this star *(right)* shimmer. The sawtooth border is exact and the feather quilting is extremely fine. Elizabeth made this quilt for her grandson Chester Neff. His initials and the date are embroidered on the back.

Eight-Pointed Star *(left)*
72 x 88
Cotton
1858
Fulton County, Ohio
Quiltmaker: Elizabeth Rufenacht
Owner: Reo Rufenacht

Lone Star *(right)*
79 x 80
Cotton
1912
Lancaster County, Pennsylvania
Quiltmaker: Elizabeth (Lizzie) Neff
Owners: Richard and Betty Neff
Pellman

Lone Star with Applique

84 x 84
Cotton
circa 1900
Lancaster County, Pennsylvania
Quiltmaker: Amanda K. Nolt
Privately owned

When Amanda Nolt decided to make a quilt for her daughter, she chose a stunning, elaborate pattern. The star, consisting of hundreds of tiny diamond-shaped pieces, is wrapped by a bright red border. Surrounding the pieced star are beautiful applique flowers and plumes. Concerned for its safekeeping, Amanda's daughter stored the quilt in a chest until she passed it on to her own daughter.

Effective use of color makes this star seem to pulsate. The fine piecework in both the star and the sawtooth border, as well as close, even quilting, demonstrate the experience and skill of the makers, a mother-daughter team (the mother and grandmother of the current owner).

Lone Star

83 x 83

Cotton

circa 1925

Elkhart County, Indiana

Quiltmakers: Harriet Blosser and
*   Clara Weaver*

Owner: Thelma Yoder

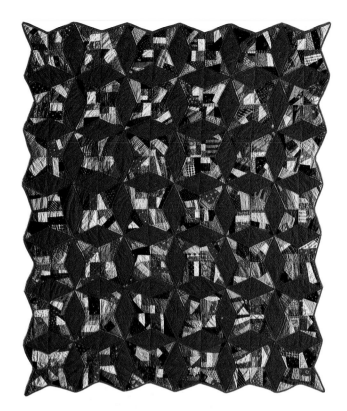

Crazy Stars *(left)*
72 x 90
Cotton
circa 1930-1955
Mifflin County, Pennsylvania
Quiltmakers: Patches done by Anna
Mary King Hartzler; finished by
Mamie K. Hartzler
Owner: Beryl Hartzler Brubaker

Colonial Star *(right)*
86 x 98
Cotton
circa 1900
Lancaster County, Pennsylvania
Quiltmaker: Elizabeth D. Leaman
Privately owned

Anna Mary King Hartzler pieced the cone-shaped sections of this quilt *(left)* but never finished it. Years later, her son searched the Montgomery Ward store for a fabric to put between the patches so his wife could finish the quilt. He chose a deep red and his wife approved! She set the patches together, quilted and bound the edges of the quilt. It was passed on to their daughter at Christmastime, 1970.

Feather quilting fills both the border and sashing of this precisely pieced quilt *(right)*. The quilt remains in the hands of the quiltmaker's family three generations later.

The red crosses on each patch provide an overall unity for the small scrap stars of this quilt. Navy blue fabric seems an appropriate setting for the bright stars.

LeMoyne Star with Cross
81 x 92
Cotton
circa 1890
McPherson County, Kansas
Quiltmaker: Mary Bontrager Yoder
Owner: Jana Gerber

Lone Star
80 x 83
Cotton
circa 1900
Lancaster County, Pennsylvania
Quiltmaker: Barbara Denlinger
Owners: Ira L. and Rhoda Mae Rutt

Ira and Rhoda Mae Rutt bought this quilt at Rhoda's mother's public sale. Rhoda's grandmother made this well pieced quilt that is covered with feather stitching.

Ben and Kate Leaman took a teamwork approach to quiltmaking. Ben cut the patches and Kate sewed them together. They intended to make quilts for each of their grandchildren. Elsie, the 19th grandchild, received this quilt *(left)*. The couple suffered failing health, however, before they were able to make quilts for their youngest six or seven grandchildren.

Elsie, a young girl at the time she received her quilt, placed it in her hope chest where it stayed until her marriage in 1946. When she and her husband hosted company on Sundays, she would take the quilt out and put it on the spare room bed. Their house had no coat closet on the first floor, so guests took their coats to the spare bedroom and placed them on the bed, where they could see and admire Elsie's lovely quilt.

Diamond Star (left)
82 x 84
Cotton
1924
Lancaster County, Pennsylvania
Quiltmakers: Kate and Ben Leaman
Owner: Elsie Marie Leaman Beachey

Most Lone Star quilts are pieced with diamond-shaped pieces. This one *(right)* uses strips instead. Catherine's grandson is the current owner of this quilt, which has never been used.

Lone Star (right)
73 x 73
Cotton
circa 1910
Montgomery County, Pennsylvania
Quiltmaker: Catherine Beidler
Owner: Willard B. Beidler

Katie Graber Tieszen, who encouraged Maria Vogt in her quiltmaking, is shown here in 1960 with her husband.

Maria Vogt, of German origin, immigrated from Russia to South Dakota where she settled in a small town with her daughter. Maria's husband died at a relatively young age, leaving the woman and her daughter to a somewhat secluded and austere lifestyle.

Maria was an excellent seamstress and did fine handwork. A neighbor, Katie Graber Tieszen, admired her craftsmanship and befriended Maria. Katie's fluency in German made it easy for her and Maria to communicate.

Katie was the mother of six children. Her youngest daughter, Ruby, remembers that they called Maria "Tante Vogtia," a title showing respect for this friend of their mother. Ruby remembers being disturbed, as a child, by Tante Vogtia's appearance. A tall, stately woman, she dressed in black from top to toe and carried a black umbrella to shield herself from both sunshine and rain.

Katie's husband, a chiropractor by profession, was often visited by traveling suit salesmen, who carried books of wool fabric swatches appropriate for tailored suits. They customarily left these swatches with their customers. Katie collected them, then hired Maria to make them into quilts. Maria produced several quilts for the family in various patterns, but each carried her fine feather embroidery stitches in various colors.

Fan
65 x 82
Wool
1937
Turner County, South Dakota
Quiltmaker: Maria Vogt
Owner: Ruby Tieszen Waltner

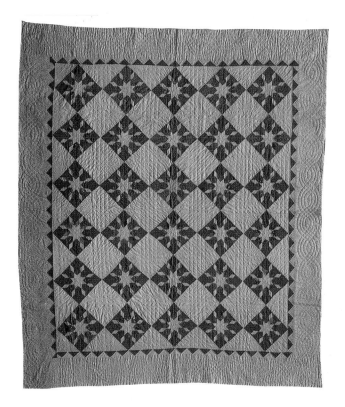

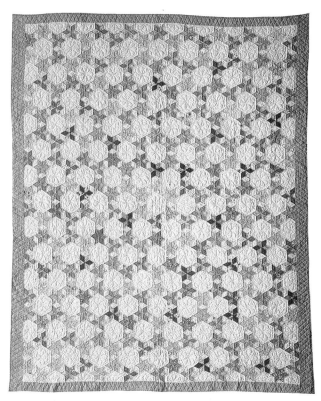

Blazing Star (left)
70 x 79
Cotton
circa 1890
Holmes County, Ohio
Quiltmaker: Mary Horner Yakely
Owner: Beth Martin Birky

Mary Horner Yakely made this quilt *(left)* for her daughter Sara Edna Yakely, who was born in 1879. Edna married Levi Gardner in 1902. She gave the quilt to her only daughter, Erma Gardner Mast, born in 1913. Erma prized the quilt and never used it except to display it at times in her guest room.

Erma had three daughters—a fact which presented her with a problem about who should inherit the family quilt! Erma's oldest daughter, Betty Mast Martin, had only one daughter, Beth.

When Beth was engaged to be married, Erma asked her to select a pattern for a wedding quilt, a gift Erma gave each grandchild. Beth had always liked the antique quilt and requested a reproduction of it. Erma decided instead to give Beth the original old quilt at the time of her wedding on November 24, 1984. She also made a new quilt of the same pattern so Beth could preserve the heirloom and still have a quilt to use. The original quilt is now in the hands of the great-great-grand-daughter of the maker.

Stars (right)
70 x 87
Cotton
circa 1935
Bureau County, Illinois
Quiltmaker: Phoebe Smith Schmidt
        Bachman
Owner: Carolyn Shank (Mrs.
        Kenneth Shank)

The maker of this quilt *(right)* likely used scraps, and then supplemented them with solid colors to make the dozens of small stars that comprise this quilt. It is entirely hand-stitched, except for the binding which has been machine-stitched on one side and hand-stitched on the other.

The current owner of the quilt is a great-granddaughter of its maker.

Heavy wool fabrics make this a sturdy wintertime quilt, well suited to Canadian cold. Although the quilt was made to be used only by "company," it appears that guests came either in the summertime or elected not to use it. The quilt shows little wear.

Strip Stars
72 x 83
Wool
circa 1919
York County, Ontario, Canada
Quiltmaker: Elizabeth Reesor
*   Wideman*
Owner: Ruth Wideman Reesor

Lone Star

85 x 85
Cotton
1901
Franconia, Montgomery County,
     Pennsylvania
Quiltmaker: Mrs. Nathaniel Lewis
     Willouer
Owner: Mennonite Historians of
     Eastern Pennsylvania,
     Harleysville, Pennsylvania

Aaron's mother made this quilt as his Christmas gift when he was 14 years old. The quilt is dated "December 25, 1901" with "Aaron Willouer" stitched carefully above the date. The quilt shows little wear; it was likely stored almost constantly in a chest.

This quilt is one in a series of five nearly identical quilts made by Rebecca Miller Reesor for her five step-grandchildren. The fabrics vary slightly in each quilt.

Dresden plate medallions in pieced circles surround the star.

Lone Star
69 x 75
Cotton
circa 1910
York County, Ontario, Canada
Quiltmaker: Rebecca Miller Reesor
Owner: Ruth Wideman Reesor

Lone Star with Sawtooth Border
(left)
78 x 80
Cotton
circa 1900
Lancaster County, Pennsylvania
Quiltmaker: Annie G. Herr Erb
Owner: Mabel Erb Nolt (Mrs. Ben
  Nolt)

Annie Erb made quilts for each of her children in preparation for their marriages. Her daughter Mabel remembers that the three older daughters each received six or seven quilts, lovingly made by their mother. The sons got fewer quilts. Mabel, who was only 16 when her mother died, treasures this quilt *(left)* as a memory of her mother.

Mabel recalls their family rising early in the morning. By 6:00 a.m. they had the cows milked and the milk cooled in large milk cans with spigots. Mabel's morning chores extended beyond barn work. While her mother pieced quilts during those early morning hours, Mabel was summoned to press seams open as sections of quilts were sewn together. This Lone Star had numerous seams to press. She did the pressing with a sad-iron heated over the stove. All of this activity preceded breakfast and young Mabel's day at school.

Lone Star with Applique *(right)*
95 x 95
Cotton
circa 1875
Montgomery County,Pennsylvania
Quiltmaker: Unknown
Owner: Mennonite Historians of
  Eastern Pennsylvania,
  Harleysville, Pennsylvania

Though it is known to have come from a Mennonite family in Souderton, Pennsylvania, this quilt *(right)* was sold at public auction and its specific history was lost. The quilt displays excellent workmanship in both piecework and the applique surrounding the star.

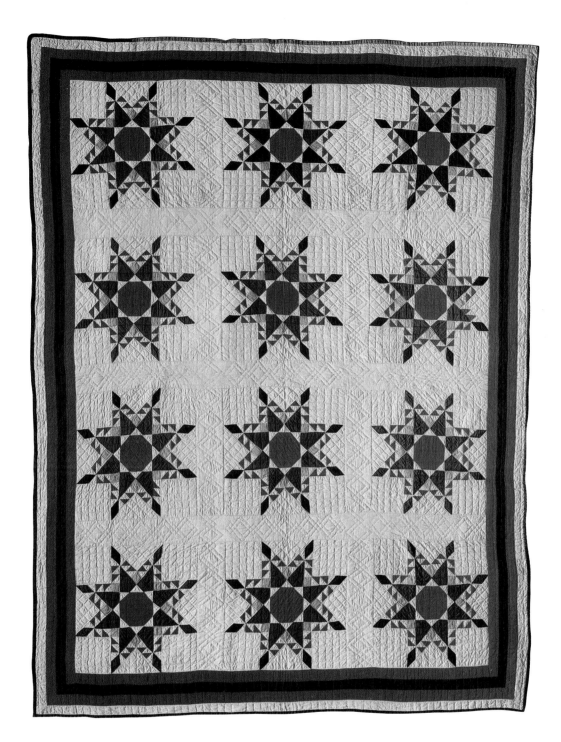

Elizabeth Naffziger and her daughters put this beautiful quilt together while living on a farm in Boynton Township, Tazewell County, Illinois. The date "1886" is embroidered in tiny stitches on the back. The quilt was donated to the Historical Society by Alice Naffziger Heiser, a niece of one of the makers, Minnie Naffziger Eichelberger.

Feathered Star

72 x 92

Cotton

1886

Tazewell County, Illinois

Quiltmaker: Elizabeth Naffziger (Mrs. Valentine F. Naffziger)and her daughters Emma, Ella and Minnie

Owner: Illinois Mennonite Historical and Genealogical Society

Lone Star

81 x 82

Cotton

1938

Lancaster County, Pennsylvania

Quiltmaker: Bertha M. Stauffer
*   Widders*

Owner: Lorraine Shirk

Bertha gave this quilt to her daughter Edith on the occasion of her marriage to John Boll in 1941. Edith used the quilt only at special times in the early years of their marriage, and then put the quilt away to preserve it. Her daughter Lorraine bought the quilt at the public auction of her parents' belongings.

Lena Zaerr was not intimidated by difficult piecing patterns or quilting designs. Each large star *(left)* has five tiny pieced stars in its interior. Elegant feather plumes are used around the stars and on the border. Lena made one of these quilts for each of her great-nieces and -nephews.

Most quilters choose a simple, uncomplicated pattern for their first quilt and then progress to more difficult designs as they gain experience. Not Fannie Good. This intricate star *(right)* is her first effort at piecing a quilt. Her success is obvious. Although this top was quilted by Pearl Suter, Fannie also mastered the art of quilting and has since taken many quilts from start to finish herself.

Feathered Star *(left)*
84 x 84
Cotton
1933
Fulton County, Ohio
Quiltmaker: Lena Zaerr
Owner: Mrs. Stella Crossgrove

Radiant Star *(right)*
71 x 84
Cotton
circa 1930
Rockingham County, Virginia
Quiltmaker: Pieced by Fannie E.
*   Good; quilted by Pearl Suter*
Owner: Fannie E. Good

Lone Star with Applique

77 x 84
Cotton
circa 1900
Waterloo County, Ontario, Canada
Quiltmaker: Annie Horst Bauman
Owner: Esther Brubacher Nafziger

As a leader in the Old Order Mennonite church in the 1800s, Annie Horst Bauman's grandfather was criticized for his worldly act of purchasing a treadle sewing machine for each of his daughters before their marriages. Annie Horst Bauman pieced this quilt on her mother's sewing machine prior to her marriage in 1902.

Both the quilt and the treadle machine are still in the family.

As the name of this pattern implies, a section cut from one fabric is replaced by a section of the same size and shape from a contrasting fabric.

Quilting motifs chosen for this example *(left)* emphasize the curves and highlight the overall pattern.

Robbing Peter to Pay Paul *(left)*
77 x 55
Cotton
circa 1925
Elkhart County, Indiana
Quiltmaker: Francis J. Yoder
Owner: Thelma Yoder

Quilted circles accent the circular visual impact established in the pieced design of this quilt *(right).* The angular lines of the sawtooth border stand in sharp contrast to the inner circles. The date "1913" and initials "MRL" are beautifully double-quilted inside two of the bottom patches. Kate made the quilt for her son Martin Rohrer Leaman. He was married in 1914 so the quilt was likely made in anticipation of his wedding.

Robbing Peter to Pay Paul *(right)*
79 x 80
Cotton
1913
Lancaster County, Pennsylvania
Quiltmaker: Katherine (Kate) Rohrer
Leaman
Privately owned

Rose Applique

75 x 94

Cotton Sateen

1937

McPherson County, Kansas

Quiltmaker: Anna Schmidt Sperling

Owner: Anne Thiessen Colvin

*(granddaughter of Anna Schmidt
        Sperling)*

Anna Schmidt was born in Harvey County, Kansas, in 1887. Her parents were both immigrants from the area of Molotschna Franzthal, Russia, having come to Kansas in 1874.

Anna married Cornelius C. Sperling in 1907. About three years after her marriage, Anna developed a series of ear infections. Antibiotic medications were not available, and resultant complications began a slow but certain decline in her ability to hear. The hearing loss became progressively worse with each of her pregnancies. By the time her fifth child, Irene, was born in 1923, Anna was completely deaf. Irene recalls that, "somehow our home was no different from anyone else's because of Mother's tremendous positive attitude, which was definitely nurtured by her strong faith in God."

Anna was a farm wife and enjoyed being outdoors. She was an active participant in caring for the cattle and sheep. In the summer she helped with the wheat harvest. But in the fall and winter she took time to catch up on sewing and quilting projects. Anna always seemed to have a quilt set up in one room of the house during the cold months.

Each roll of batting that Anna purchased for the middle layer of her quilts had a quilt pattern printed on its wrapper. Anna used many of these patterns, although she often adapted them to suit her own creative tastes. The Rose quilt shown here is one she made, inspired by a McCall's transfer pattern suggested for curtains. Anna arranged the roses on a quilt top, then surrounded them with a triple border, anchored at each corner

with a nine-patch block. The rose motif is echoed in the quilting design of the border. Prairie points in alternate shades finish the edges of the quilt.

A member of the Hoffnungsau Mennonite Church, Anna made quilts for the church's annual mission sale. She was an active participant in the church's mission society and made many quilt tops which the group quilted and donated to relief organizations. Mary Schirmer, a close friend of Anna's, worked as a missionary among the Hopi Indians in Arizona. Anna made a quilt top which she sent along with batting and backing to the Hopi women. In 1940 she had the opportunity to visit the Hopi reservation where she saw her quilt top, beautifully finished by the Hopi women.

Anna Schmidt Sperling is at the far left. Her friends, from left to right, are Elizabeth Sperling, Agatha Ediger and Marie Voth. The picture was taken in 1905. The women are wearing the dresses they made for their graduation projects after completing a sewing class in Goessel, Kansas.

Sawtooth and Square

83 x 83
Cotton
circa 1880
Washington County, Maryland
Quiltmaker: Christianna Keener
    Martin
Privately owned

Christianna made this quilt for her hope chest prior to her marriage. It is meticulously crafted, each sawtooth corner being perfectly resolved. The binding has a narrow edge of piping.

The quilt, never used and in beautiful condition, was sold at the public auction of Mrs. Martin's personal possessions. It was purchased and given to a great-niece of the quiltmaker by her parents.

Along with fancy feathers, Mary L. Landis quilted the date "1888" in the center of her quilt. The solid red and green, common fabric choices for Lancaster County quilters of this time period, provide strong contrast to the jagged sawtooth edges. Graceful feather quilting softens the strong geometric shapes.

Sawtooth Diamond

80 x 80

Cotton

1888

Lancaster County, Pennsylvania

Quiltmaker: Mary Leaman Landis

Owner: Daniel L. Wenger

Trip Around the World
78 x 80
Cotton
circa 1920
Lancaster County, Pennsylvania
Quiltmaker: Lydia Lehman
Owner: Edna H. Keener

Though it appears she used scraps for this quilt, Lydia arranged them carefully and artistically to create a pleasing balance of color and pattern.

She made the quilt for her grandson, Amos L. Keener, when he married Dorothy H. Hershey in 1927. The quilt was displayed on a bed only on special occasions.

Stitched on the back of this quilt *(left)* in red embroidery thread is this note: "This quilt was pieced in 1888 and presented to Emma J. Yoder when she left Missouri for Oregon." Emma was 14 years old when her family moved.

The quilt's history after Emma's move is uncertain. The current owner purchased it from an antique dealer in Kokomo, Indiana, in 1987. The dealer told her the quilt needed "a good Mennonite home." Evelyn and her husband researched the names on the quilt and discovered to their surprise that many of the women who autographed the quilt were relatives of theirs. No one is certain how or why the quilt made the trek from Oregon to Indiana.

It appears never to have been used.

Bear Paw *(left)*
64 x 78
Cotton
1888
Cass County, Missouri
Quiltmakers: Friends of Emma J.
*   Yoder*
Owner: Evelyn Kenagy

Prior to her marriage in 1919, Elizabeth Reesor Wideman began making quilts for her hope chest. This Bear Paw *(right)* is one of two she made to use on the spare bed during the winter season. Overnight guests were rare in the wintertime so the quilt was seldom used. Most of the time it was stored in a blanket box.

Elizabeth, born in 1895, made many quilts throughout her lifetime. She frequently donated quilts to the annual auction for relief aid held by Mennonite Central Committee in Toronto. She died in August of 1985 having done her last quilting in June of that year.

Bear Paw *(right)*
68 x 82
Wool
circa 1919
York County, Ontario, Canada
Quiltmaker: Elizabeth Reesor
*   Wideman*
Owner: Ruth Wideman Reesor

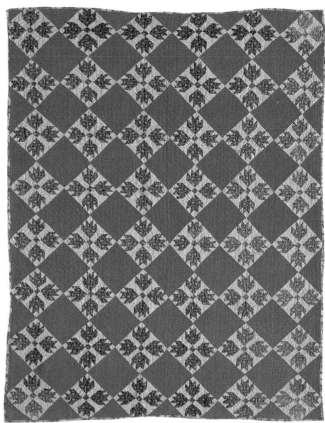

Bear Paw *(left)*
80 x 78
Cotton
1930
Reno County, Kansas
Quiltmakers: Lizzie Yutzy Kaufman
*   and her mother Emma*
*   Headings Yutzy*
Owner: Carolyn K. Hartman

Bear Paw *(right)*
65 x 85
Cotton
circa 1920
McPherson County, Kansas
Quiltmaker: Katie Krehbiel (Mrs.
*   Henry W. Krehbiel)*
Privately owned

Lizzie and her mother made this quilt *(left)* in preparation for Lizzie's marriage on December 21, 1931. The quilt was passed on to Lizzie's daughter, Carolyn, who displays it on the wall of her home.

Though this quilt *(right)* remains in the family of its creator, no further details are known about its making.

At first glance it appears that Anna may have purchased the pink, green and yellow fabrics for this quilt. Closer examination reveals a wide variety of pink and green fabrics. This quilt's "scrap" origin is neatly disguised in its careful planning.

Anna Reist Carper gave this quilt to her daughter-in-law, Eva Carper, in the early 1900s. Eva presented the treasure to her son James on the occasion of his marriage. James in turn gave the quilt as a wedding gift to his nephew, John Haines Eitzen, and bride, Kimberly Haines Eitzen.

Rolling Stone
82 x 82
Cotton
circa 1900
Lancaster County, Pennsylvania
Quiltmaker: Anna Reist Carper
Owners: John and Kimberly Haines Eitzen

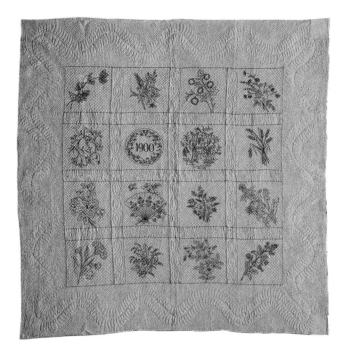

Embroidered *(left)*
72 x 72
Cotton
1900
Lancaster County, Pennsylvania
Quiltmakers: Hettie Heller Landis
and her mother and sisters
Owner: Esther Becker

Embroidered Flowers with
Picket Fence *(right)*
90 x 90
Cotton
circa 1930
Seward County, Nebraska
Quiltmaker: Magdalena (Lena)
Schlegel Kremer
Owner: DeElda Hershberger

Hettie was a great-aunt to Esther Becker. Hettie had no children of her own, and, upon her death, this quilt *(left)* was passed to Esther in 1939. Esther was a young girl at the time, but she was told that the quilt was given to her because the names Hettie and Esther have the same meaning. Esther was not expected to use the quilt but was allowed to put it on her bed when her family was having company. The visiting women admired the quilt, and Esther remembers feeling pleased to be the owner of such a beautiful treasure.

Quilts made as part of a girl's preparation for marriage were often kept in a hope chest. When company came, the women were customarily shown the girl's store of quilts.

There is a square of white fabric stitched over each corner of Hettie's quilt. This was to permit handling and showing of the quilt without fear of hands staining the corners.

DeElda Hershberger fondly remembers watching her grandmother and aunt quilt. "Quilting was something Grandma liked to do to keep busy."

The embroidered flowers on this quilt *(right)* are sheltered inside a pieced picket fence. Lest the fence seem foreboding, a gate along the bottom edge of the quilt stands ajar inviting admirers.

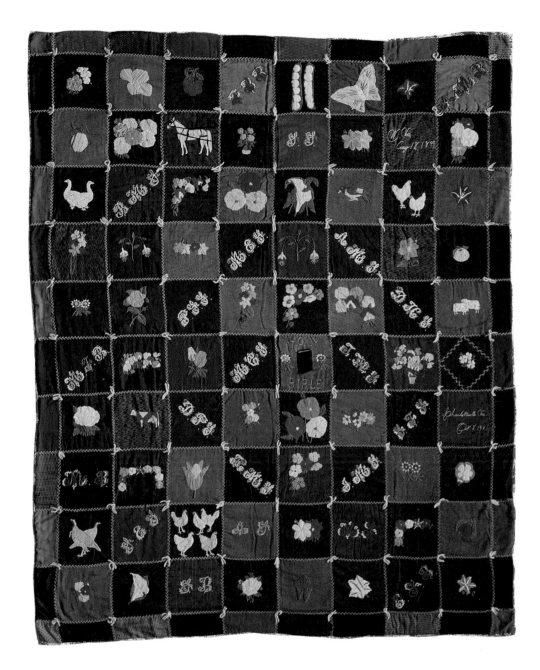

In the center of this quilt, Sophia stitched a Bible, likely symbolic of the central position it held in her life. On either side of the Bible are the initials of each of her parents. Surrounding those are the initials of the eight children in her family—four boys and four girls. Initials of her aunts and uncles are scattered elsewhere.

In August of 1899 Sophia made her first visit to West Virginia. She commemorated this event by stitching the name of the state and date of the trip into one of the patches. "Charlottesville, Virginia, Oct. 1901" is likewise remembered on another patch.

Many of the patterns were traced from seed catalogs and carefully stitched with wool thread. The images include realistic renditions of chickens, turkeys, sheep, a red and white cow, and many variations of flowers.

Crazy
66 x 79
Wool
circa 1890
Rockingham County, Virginia
Quiltmaker: Sophia Showalter
*   Brubaker*
Owners: Mary and Anna Brubaker

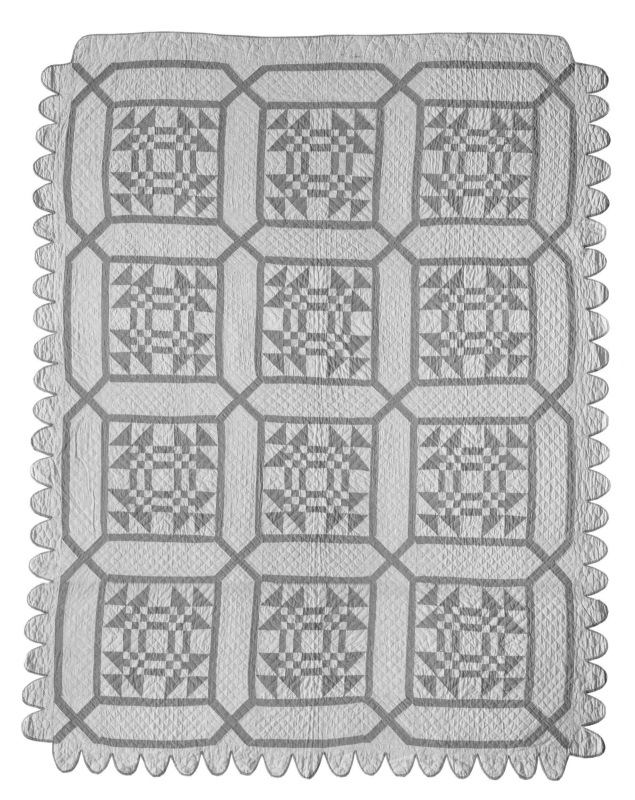

Goose in the Pond
72 x 87
Cotton
1918
Elkhart County, Indiana
Quiltmaker: Ella Berkey Litwiller
Owner: Sara Yoder Von Gunten

Ella Berkey Litwiller made this quilt for her daughter Lillian Litwiller Yoder as a high school graduation present.

Lillian came home from school during the noon recess on November 11, 1918 to find the living room full of her mother's friends, busily working on her quilt. While she was there, the phone rang one long ring. The central phone office in Middlebury had a message for the town. The long ring signaled that all persons sharing the "party line" should pick up the phone. The message from the operator was, "The war in Europe is over." Lillian remembers that the women seated at the quilting frame jumped from their chairs and danced around the room.

The pattern of the quilt, though simple, required care and precision to achieve its clean sharp lines. Each patch is surrounded by strips of sashing, creating a garden maze pattern. The edging is a series of severe scallops, each curve even and each point sharp. The top edge of the quilt was left straight.

The quilt now belongs to Lillian's daughter Sara.

Lillian Litwiller Yoder was the recipient of this quilt made by her mother. This picture of Lillian was taken in 1919 when she graduated from Middlebury (Indiana) High School.

Crazy
68 x 78
Wool and cotton
1893
Garden City, Missouri
Quiltmakers: Women of Sycamore
*   Grove Mennonite Church*
Owner: Virginia Grove Weaver

Mary Alice ("Mollie") and Lewis ("L.J.") Heatwole moved from Harrisonburg, Virginia, to Garden City, Missouri, in 1890. L.J. served as pastor in the local Mennonite church for a short period before he and Mollie moved back to Virginia. The women of the church presented this quilt to L.J. when he visited several years later, with instructions to take it back to their friend Mollie as a token of their love.

The crazy patches here are hexagons rather than squares and are embellished with traditional fancy stitching, as well as unusual embroidered animals, birds and flowers. The date "1903" is also embroidered on one patch. The quiltmaker was the owner's great-grandmother.

Crazy
69 x 74
Wool and cotton
1903
Elkhart County, Indiana
Quiltmaker: Harriet Blosser
Owner: Susan E. Yoder

 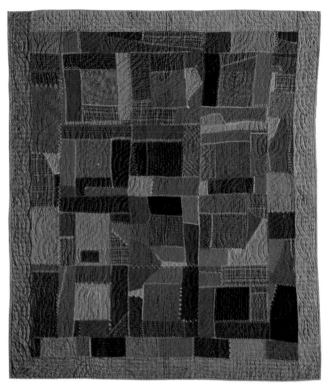

Crazy *(left)*
67 x 79
Wool, cotton and silk
circa 1900
Cottonwood County, Minnesota
Quiltmaker: Elizabeth Harder
Owner: Becky J. Harder

Crazy *(right)*
72 x 82
Wool and cotton
circa 1910
Stephenson County, Illinois
Quiltmaker: Elizabeth Brubaker
        Shoemaker (Mrs. J. S.
        Shoemaker)
Owner: Evelyn Shoemaker Miller

A variety of fabrics and decorative stitchery combine to make this a unique and beautiful quilt *(left)*. Becky Harder was a young child when her grandmother Elizabeth died. She never really learned to know this grandmother who had moved to the United States from Russia in the 1870s.

Elizabeth Shoemaker was adept at the art of Crazy quilts *(right)*. She covered each seam with fancy embroidery in a variety of styles. She quilted wide vertical cables in the center part of the quilt and used a fan quilting motif on the borders.

Elizabeth made a Crazy quilt for each of her nine children. This one was given to her son C. B. Shoemaker of Scottdale, Pennsylvania. He kept it in a chest in the attic until passing it onto his daughter Evelyn after her marriage to C. Nevin Miller.

The central circle motif, around which fan patches are assembled to create a sphere, is a fitting symbol for a Friendship quilt. Neighbors of Ira Christophel autographed scraps of fabric that were then converted to crazy patches and joined to create a delightful quilt and memory.

Crazy

72 x 71

Wool, cotton and silk

1921

Elkhart County, Indiana

Quiltmakers: Neighbors of Ira
        Christophel

Owners: James and Mary Martin
        Christophel

Crazy *(left)*
72 x 75
Cotton and rayon
1925—piecing; 1945—quilting
York County, Ontario, Canada
Quiltmaker: Elizabeth Barkey Reesor
Owner: Mrs. Elizabeth Bearinger

In the year 1925, when Elizabeth Barkey Reesor was 90 years old and living in the *dawdi-haus*, a great-granddaughter was born in the main house and named Elizabeth. Great-grandmother Reesor decided to make a quilt *(left)* for her namesake.

A niece, Fanny Wilson, was a milliner and gave Elizabeth a bundle of lining patches which she cut up and hand-pieced into crazy patches.

The top remained unquilted until 1945 when great-granddaughter Elizabeth and her mother decided to quilt it. They marked the quilting design as they had seen Great-grandma do it. She took a length of string and tied knots in it at equal intervals. Placing the end of the string at one corner of the quilt, she held a pencil or piece of chalk on one knot, and then swung the string from side to side to form a fan pattern. She repeated that process by moving the pencil or chalk from knot to knot.

Crazy *(right)*
81 x 84
Cotton and wool
1900
Lancaster County, Pennsylvania
Quiltmaker: Bertha Kreider
      Denlinger (Mrs. Benjamin
      Denlinger)
Owner: R. Elverta Denlinger (Mrs.
      Roy Denlinger)

Bertha quilted her initials and the date among the patches of the center square of this Crazy quilt *(right)*. Each patch in the quilt has a design quilted on it. The motifs include flowers, leaves, feather-like shapes, crescents, acorns, grapes and other abstract shapes. All appear to have been drawn freehand by the quilter.

This was a special quilt and was handled that way. When the quilt was given to Elverta it appeared to have had little use. She put it on a spare bed until discovering that the sun was fading its borders. She placed it in a chest again to protect its beauty.

During the 1920s Adam and Sarah Schumacher made several trips to Oregon where they established friendships. Daughters Susan and Lydia decided to make a friendship quilt as a gift to their parents. They solicited patches from friends in Ohio and Oregon and eventually received 64 patches. The Oregonians listed their names and home towns on the blocks they submitted. The daughters created the quilt, and then presented this symbol of community to their parents.

Friendship

73 X 73

Cotton

circa 1930

Wayne County, Ohio

Quiltmakers: Susan Schumacher
    Gerber and Lydia Ann
    Schumacher Zimmerly

Owner: June E. Bixler

Friendship Sampler

84 x 85

Cotton

circa 1897

Berks County, Pennsylvania

Quiltmaker: Mary Gehman Kriebel

Owner: Mennonite Historians of
Eastern Pennsylvania,
Harleysville, Pennsylvania

Mary Gehman must have been a popular young woman. When she decided to make a friendship quilt, 102 friends responded with patches. That was too many for one quilt, so she made two. The larger (containing 61 patches) is shown above. The smaller quilt (41 patches) remains in the hands of Mary's daughter.

After collecting the blocks from her friends, Mary took them to her cousin Daniel G. Gehman, a printer in Bally, Pennsylvania. Daniel printed the names and any additional sentiments in bold, print letters. He added his name and the year to a triangular block at the top of the quilt.

Mary later married John Schultz Kriebel, of the Schwenkfelder church. He joined the Mennonite church after their marriage in 1914.

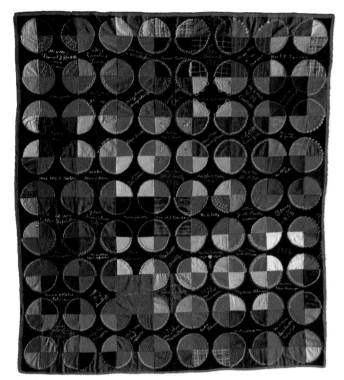 

This quilt *(left)* was presented to LaVeta Habegger's grandparents, Barbara (Bixler) and Albert E. Loganbill for their 25th wedding anniversary.

A true example of friendship, the pieces that compose this quilt were distributed to friends and relatives of Barbara and Albert so they could embroider their names on the patches to create a personalized statement of love.

This quilt continues to play an active role in keeping family connections alive. A few years ago, LaVeta traveled to Ohio with a list of the 91 names on the quilt. She was able to establish contact with a few of her grandmother's cousins who had lived more than 90 years.

She made other more circuitous links. When LaVeta and her family lived in Wichita, they hosted a young woman who had spent most of her life in Africa. Together they discovered this young woman's grandmother's name was on the quilt. Her parents were missionaries, but her grandmother had attended the Sonnenberg Mennonite Church in Kidron, Ohio, and had embroidered a patch for the Loganbills.

Mill Wheel *(left)*
86 x 76
Wool, cotton and silk
1916
Kidron, Wayne County, Ohio
Quiltmakers: Ninety-one relatives and
*   friends of Barbara (Bixler) and*
*   Albert E. Loganbill*
Owner: LaVeta Habegger

Making friendship quilts was a common custom in the late 19th and early 20th centuries. Young women distributed patches to their friends who signed the patches in some way, then returned them to the givers who incorporated them into quilt tops. Sometimes the women were asked to piece or applique the patches.

Marie Zerger gave squares of muslin to 30 friends and invited them to decorate them in whatever way they wished. Marie died in her early 30s; her quilt appears to have never been used. It is still in the possession of her family.

Friendship *(right)*
69 x 81
Cotton
1924
McPherson County, Kansas
Quiltmaker: Marie Zerger
Privately owned

Log Cabin
80 x 80
Cotton
circa 1900
Lancaster County, Pennsylvania
Quiltmaker: Sarah Diener Kennel
Privately owned

Sarah made this quilt and gave it to her daughter Kate Kennel Yost before Kate's wedding in 1909. The quilt has been handed down through the generations.

Many of the Log Cabin blocks in this quilt are made with all black fabric, but of different varieties. It is those black variations that create the shimmering energy in this quilt.

Annie Horst Bauman was Old Order Mennonite, and therefore did not wear the bright colors used in the quilt. Yet her love for these colors is obvious in her skillful blending of them.

Annie was married in 1902; the border of the quilt is made from the skirt of her navy blue wedding dress. The exact date of the quilt is unknown.

Log Cabin
67 x 79
Cotton and silk
circa 1910
Waterloo County, Ontario, Canada
Quiltmakers: Annie Horst Bauman
*   with help from her sister-in-law,*
*   Molly Bauman*
Owner: Esther Brubacher Nafziger

Quiltmaker Phoebe Sarah Sears shown with her husband Charles Wilson Culp around the time of their marriage on January 7, 1903.

Science Ridge Mennonite Church in Sterling, Illinois, was the home of an active sewing circle. Women from all stages of life attended—newlyweds to grandmothers. They met together once a month to sew, make comforters and do other projects which were sent to areas of the world in need. Over time, the women became good friends and decided to make friendship quilts for each other. The idea blossomed in 1930, "the year the banks closed," remembers Mildred Mellinger, one of the participants. They briefly questioned the wisdom of taking on the project but concluded it was worth doing, despite the hard economic times.

They first needed to decide which pattern each of the 20 women would make, so as to avoid having any duplicate patches. Each woman was assigned to do 20 patches of the one pattern she chose and to autograph each one. At subsequent monthly meetings the women exchanged their finished blocks until each had gathered 20 different patches. Each individual then chose sashing and border fabrics and assembled her quilt top. This step gave each quilt its own personality.

Then came the quilting. Most of the quilts were quilted in the homes of the owners. If a member's home could not accommodate a quilting frame, the quilt was set up and quilted in the church basement. To keep from burdening the hostess, each woman attending brought a dish for lunch, adding variety and surprise to each occasion. One woman, unveiling her contribution to the meal, proudly announced that she had brought something they hadn't had for a long time, something she was sure they'd all be glad for. She opened her container to reveal deviled eggs, only to discover that two other women had had the same inspiration that day!

Several years passed before all 20 quilts were finished. The completion date was added to each as it was done. The participants in this project were: Phoebe Sears Culp, Marie Conrad, Jennie Kreider, Lorene Henderson, Bettie Brunk, Anna Myers, Mamie Ebersole, Mattie Shore, Ada Nunemaker, Lena Landis, Addie Landis, Esther Nunemaker, Eliza Book, Mildred Mellinger, Mamie Good, Bertha Landis, Anna Shank, Anna Bare, Lizzie Lefevre and Cora Hartzler.

Friendship Sampler
76 x 94
1933
Whiteside, Illinois
Quiltmakers: Phoebe Sears Culp and
*   friends*
Owner: Sarah Buller Fenton

Log Cabin *(left)*
86 x 86
Cotton
circa 1925
Rockwell City, Iowa
Quiltmaker: Fannie Kaufman
*   Kemmerer*
Owner: Lola M. Kauffmann

Log Cabin *(right)*
76 x 76
Cotton
circa 1924
Lancaster County, Pennsylvania
Quiltmaker: Anna Martin
Privately owned

When Bessie Kaufman Good wrote to her Aunt Fannie Kaufman Kemmerer in the late 1920s, apologizing for something she said to her a few years earlier, Fannie sent Bessie this quilt in reply. Bessie did not use the quilt, but each spring and fall she hung it and other stored items outside on the washline to "air." Bessie's daughter Lola always commented on how much she liked the quilt. When Lola grew up, her mother gave it to her. Lola uses the quilt only on special occasions.

Anna Martin made this quilt *(right)*, and then gave it to her namesake granddaughter, Anna Weaver Sensenig, soon after she was born. Anna Sensenig cherished the quilt, and after she was grown, used it carefully for her own family. However, one day after being washed and hung outdoors on the washline to dry, the quilt fell victim to one of the family dogs who chewed a corner of the quilt. Anna salvaged the quilt and stored it from then on in a blanket chest for safekeeping.

Mary made this quilt for her daughter, Elizabeth B. Leaman Keener, prior to her marriage. Elizabeth's maiden initials, "E.L.," are stitched on one end. She was married October 27, 1887. The quilt was passed on to Betty (Mary Elizabeth) Keener Drescher because she was named after her grandmother.

Pineapple Log Cabin
90 x 94
Cotton
circa 1887
Lancaster County, Pennsylvania
Quiltmaker: Mary Brubaker
*   Leaman (Mrs. Benjamin Leaman)*
Owner: Mary Elizabeth (Betty)
*   Keener Drescher*

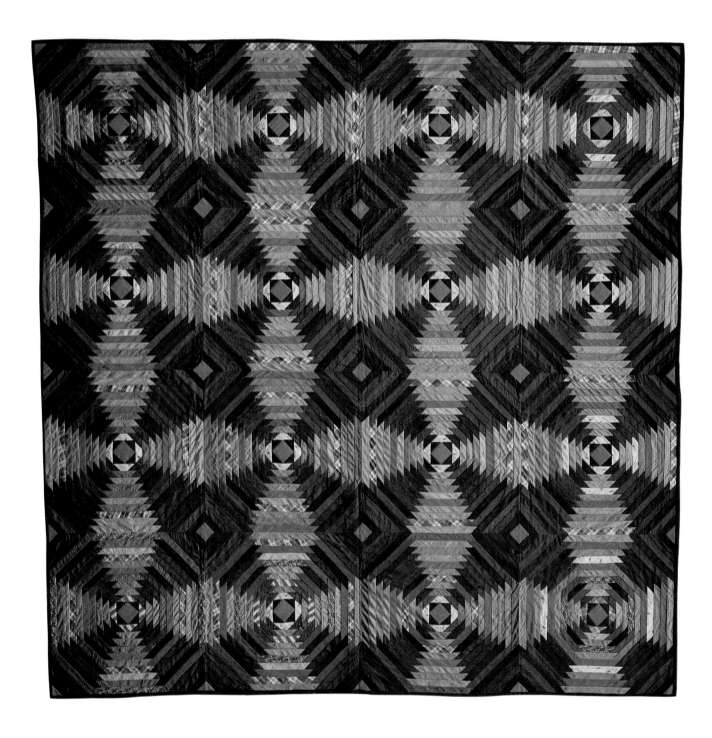

Log Cabin
91 x 93
Wool and cotton
circa 1888
Lancaster County, Pennsylvania
Quiltmaker: Uncertain—possibly
Amanda Hersh
Owner: Becky Longenecker

Now in the hands of the third generation of its maker, this quilt is a family heirloom. The family believes that the quilt was made for or by Mrs. Amanda Hersh at the time of her marriage in 1888. Amanda and her husband were members of Kraybill Mennonite Church. Amanda passed the quilt on to her daughter Mrs. Kathryn Longenecker, who passed it on to her daughter Becky.

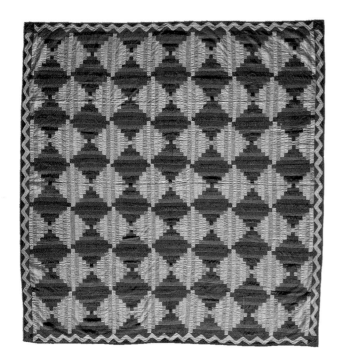

Norman and Katie Kulp received this quilt *(left)* from Norman's mother Amanda when they were married in 1914. The quilt is distinguished by its zigzag border, which is considerably more difficult to piece than the comparatively simple Log Cabin pattern.

Norman and Katie did not use the quilt. They preserved it carefully, and when their son Floyd married Gladys in 1939, they handed the quilt on to the next generation.

Grandmother Lizzie lived with her son and his family. In fact, grandson Paul remembers Lizzie as a "second mother." As she aged, Lizzie became ill and her hands became crippled. Despite that, she began to make rugs, sewing and braiding the fabrics. After rugmaking, she started making quilts. Paul remembers cut strips of fabric lying across her bed as she carefully planned her colorful quilts. Lizzie's wool fabrics came from her brother-in-law, James Gable, who owned and operated a large wool factory in Marlboro, Massachusetts. She chose only fabrics of comparable quality so the quilts would not wear unevenly.

Paul's wife, Ann, remembers being struck by the beauty of this quilt *(right)* as it hung on the clothesline for its semi-annual airing. When finished, the quilt was carefully folded, placed in a muslin flour sack, and returned to the cedar chest.

Paul and Ann acquired the quilt when the family divided Paul's parents' possessions after their deaths. Paul and Ann use it for special guests.

Log Cabin *(left)*
80 x 86
Cotton
circa 1914
Montgomery County, Pennsylvania
Quiltmaker: Amanda Landis Kulp
       (Mrs. Simon C. Kulp)
Owners: Floyd and Gladys Kulp

Log Cabin *(right)*
88 x 90
Wool
1935
Lancaster County, Pennsylvania
Quiltmaker: Lizzie Bausman Gingrich
Owners: Paul and Ann Gingrich

Tulip Applique *(left)*

81 x 92

Cotton

1933

McPherson County, Kansas

Quiltmaker: Anna Schmidt Sperling

Owner: Irene Sperling Thiessen

Floral Applique *(right)*

71 x 74

Cotton

1927

Elkhart County, Indiana

Quiltmaker: Lottie Weaver Ramer

Owner: Phyllis Ramer Garber

Anna Schmidt Sperling enjoyed the challenge of modifying a printed quilt pattern to create her own original design *(left)*. Her daughter remembers that she used only Mountain Mist batting, which always carried a quilt pattern on its wrapping. Though Anna used many of these patterns, her quilts usually included adaptations in pattern and color, making her quilts truly unique.

Lottie made this quilt *(right)* for her son Clifford at the time of his wedding. Clifford's wife died within several years and he remarried, bringing the quilt to that marriage also. Clifford's daughter Phyllis remembers that she was so happy when guests came and her mother put this special quilt on the bed.

Clifford died in 1974. When his widow moved to a smaller apartment, she sold the furniture and household goods to her seven children. Phyllis purchased the quilt at that time for $.50.

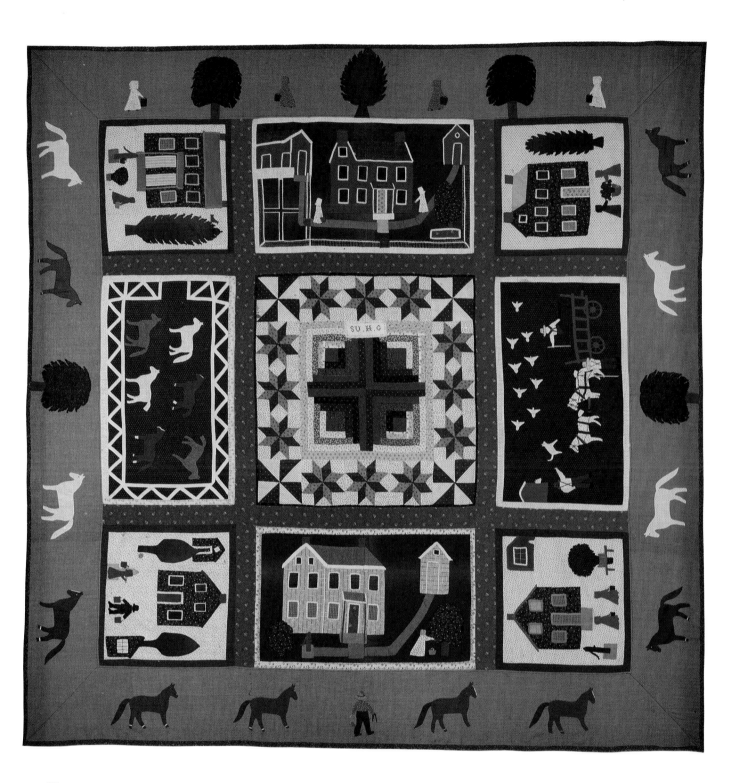

Susanna appliqued the scenes she saw from her porch, thus capturing many farm chores on the patches of this exquisite quilt. She made the quilt for her granddaughter Susie, Mrs. Phares M. Martin.

Applique
77 x 77
Cotton
circa 1910
Lancaster County, Pennsylvania
Quiltmaker: Susanna Martin Gehman
Owner: The Lancaster Mennonite
        Conference Historical Society

Bleeding Heart
79 x 79
Cotton
circa 1885
Franklin County, Pennsylvania
Quiltmaker: Mary Ann (Molly) Grove
Privately owned

Molly Grove spent many hours on this expertly appliqued and finely quilted masterpiece. Each little berry is perfectly round, the swag border is uniform and even, and the patches are exact and symmetrical.

Molly made the quilt for her hope chest. However, before marriage, her boyfriend rejected her and she never married. The quilt remained stored in a chest until it was sold, along with Molly's other personal possessions at a public auction. Molly's first cousin purchased the quilt and passed it on to her daughter.

60

Catharine Diener made a quilt for each of her daughters, intending that each pass hers on to her daughter, specifically, the daughter named Catharine! In the event that there was no daughter by that name, the quilt was to be given to the eldest daughter! This quilt was given to the oldest daughter of Sarah Diener Kennel, born in 1881. Her name, after her grandmother, was Catharine (Kate) Kennel Yost.

Whig Rose
82 x 83
Cotton
circa 1870
Lancaster County, Pennsylvania
Quiltmaker: Catharine Diener
Privately owned

Sunlight and Shadows

84 x 84
Cotton
circa 1890
Lancaster County, Pennsylvania
Quiltmaker: Anna Hess Heller
Owner: Holly Blosser Yoder

At the turn of the century in Lancaster County, Pennsylvania, young people usually married before they joined the Mennonite church. Church members dressed in "plain clothing," prescribed by the church and, usually, dramatically different from what these persons had worn before.

Anna E. Hess (1851-1926) married Benjamin Denlinger Heller in 1873, and together they joined the Landis Valley Mennonite Church. Anna packed her pins, beads, gold rings, and fancy clothing into a chest made by her father, Samuel Risser Hess. The chest also contained her penmanship copy books, some old

This family portrait shows Anna E. Hess Heller, maker of the quilt. Laura, the only daughter, shown here at age 11 with her six brothers, was the recipient of the quilt.

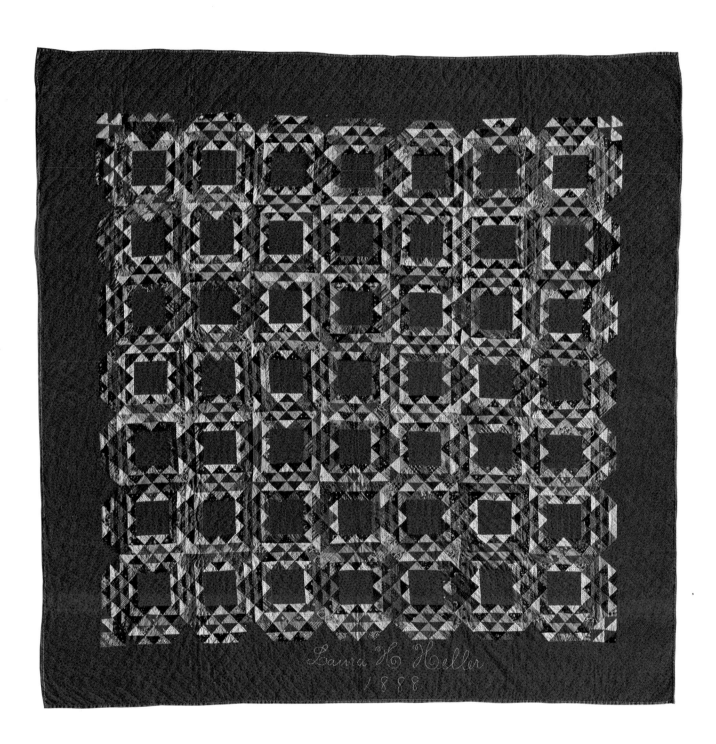

Ocean Waves

80 x 80

Cotton

1888

Lancaster County, Pennsylvania

Quiltmaker: Anna Hess Heller

Owner: Anna Heller Fager Blosser

letters and miscellaneous memorabilia.

Ben and Anna became the parents of six sons and one daughter. They lived on a farm. Along with domestic and farm chores, Anna made quilts. Several of them were stored in the chest instead of being used on beds. Among them was one she made for her two-year-old daughter Laura in 1888.

Laura's daughter Anna knew from the time she was a little girl, that she (her grandma's namesake) would someday be given the treasured chest. When Anna moved to Florida to teach school, she met Laverne Blosser, a transplanted Iowan who attended the same Mennonite church. They were married in October of 1955 and eventually moved to a farm in Iowa.

During their first year in Iowa, and while they were expecting their first child, Anna and Laverne received a special gift from her parents. Elmer Martin, a church acquaintance from Pennsylvania, made regular trips to the West in a big truck to pick up hogs. He brought the Iowa-raised hogs back to Martin's Meats for butchering. Anna's parents struck a deal with Elmer. Into the back of Elmer's truck went the family heirloom chest, along with a playpen for the coming baby. Elmer drove his truck directly to Anna and Laverne's farm where he unloaded it, then continued on his mission to pick up hogs.

As a little girl, Anna and her brothers were forbidden to open the chest (although she admits they sneaked a peek occasionally). Now it was hers and she carefully examined its treasures. Among them were these quilts.

Anna's first child, a daughter born in 1956, was named Laura after her grandmother. Laura, now grown, will be the recipient of the quilt made for the woman whose namesake she is. Laura named her daughter Anna, born in 1984, thus continuing the matrilineal line of five generations of Anna and Laura.

This chest was made in 1871 by Samuel Risser Hess for his daughter Anna Elsworth Hess. Anna married Benjamin Denlinger Heller in 1873 and made the Ocean Waves quilt for her daughter Laura.

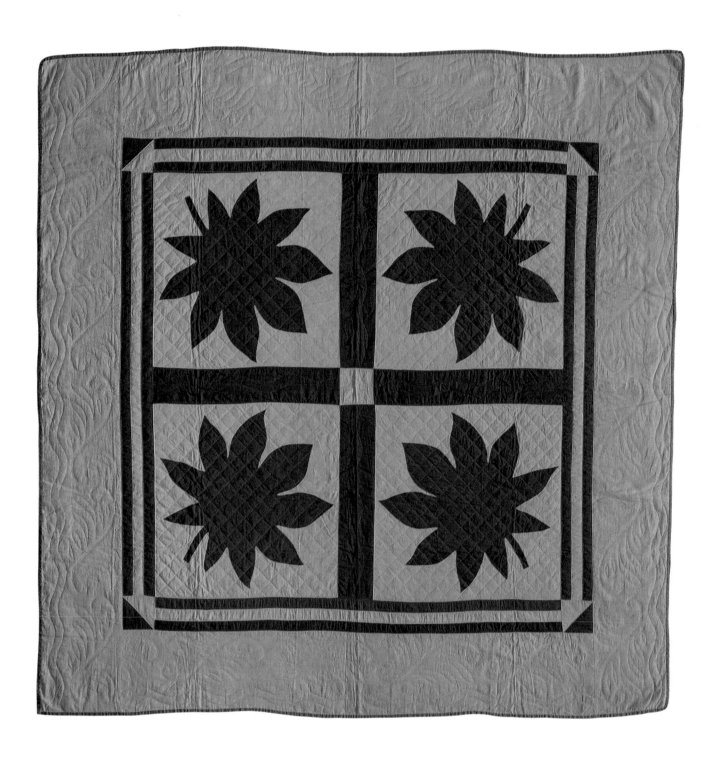

Castor Oil Bean Leaf Applique
84 x 88
Cotton
circa 1900
Lancaster County, Pennsylvania
Quiltmaker: Hannah Gehman
Privately owned

Hannah traced a leaf from the castor oil plant for her unusual applique pattern. (The leaf is actual size.) Bold sashing and a split inner border frame the leaves. Triangles at each corner create an illusion of the corners being folded in. The quilt remains in Hannah Gehman's family.

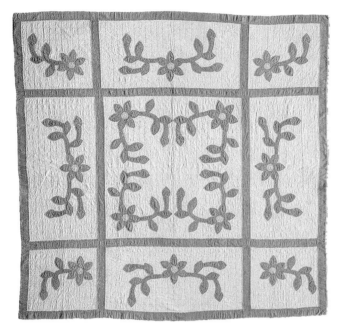

Anna Metzler visited her daughter, Elsie Metzler Lehman, one day and asked if she could spare any old feed sacks. Elsie was able to give her a supply, and her mother went home satisfied.

Anna dyed some of the fabric pink and some green and returned the feed sacks to her daughter, transformed into this applique quilt *(left)*. It is now cherished by Anna's great-granddaughter.

Martha Schneider and her mother Lena Wiens both loved quiltmaking. Lena hand-appliqued the tops, and then she and her daughter quilted them together. Martha's daughter Lovella remembers that they used only Mountain Mist batting and often duplicated the patterns shown on the plastic wrapping of the roll of batting.

This quilt *(right)* was not made for any particular reason or person—just for the family, to be eventually handed down to children and grandchildren.

Floral Applique (left)
75 x 80
Cotton
circa 1930
Mahoning, Ohio
Quiltmaker: Anna Metzler
Owner: Alice Hill

Rose of Sharon (left)
76 x 94
Cotton
circa 1930
Reno County, Kansas
Quiltmakers: Martha Schneider (Mrs.
*   Sam Schneider) and Lena Wiens*
*   (Mrs. Peter Wiens)*
Owner: Lovella Schneider Goering
*   (Mrs. Joe W. Goering)*

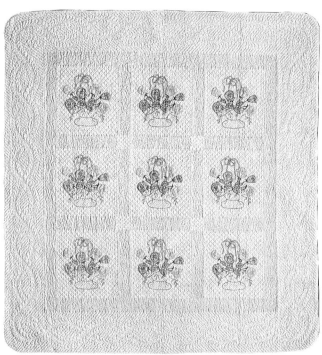

Dogwood *(left)*
75 x 88
Cotton
1941
Logan County, Ohio
Quiltmaker: Kathryn (Katie) Yoder
(Mrs. John I. Yoder)
Owner: Olive Yoder

Basket of Roses *(right)*
78 x 89
Cotton
circa 1940
Lancaster County, Pennsylvania
Quiltmakers: Applique by Hilda
Yoder; quilted by Leah Yoder
and friends
Owner: Naomi E. Yoder

When Katie Yoder's children married and moved away from home, they took tangible evidence of their mother's love and support with them. Katie made this quilt *(left)* and several others like it as wedding gifts for her children.

Sam Yoder and his bride Naomi received this quilt *(right)* when they were married in 1944. Sam's sister Hilda did all the minute applique and embroidery work. Sam's mother Leah then invited family and friends in to do the fancy quilting, which complements the applique designs.

The connection between Hannah Custer and Nancy Lehman is unknown. They have left tribute to their friendship in large applique letters splashed across the top of this quilt. Primitive folk-art style birds peck berries from a basket at the lower edge of the quilt, and bold, bright florals adorn its center section.

Whig Rose Variation

68 x 85

Cotton

1862

Somerset County, Pennsylvania

Quiltmakers: Hannah Custer and
*   Nancy Lehman*

Privately owned

President's Wreath
80 x 80
Cotton
circa 1890
Lancaster County, Pennsylvania
Quiltmaker: Mrs. Mary Herr
Haverstick
Owner: Elizabeth Herr Hess
Denlinger (Mrs. Lloyd Denlinger)

Mary Herr Haverstick, born in 1869, was an accomplished seamstress by her early twenties, as evidenced in this carefully appliqued quilt. She gave the quilt to her niece who passed it on to her daughter. The quilt was used only to decorate a bed when guests were expected.

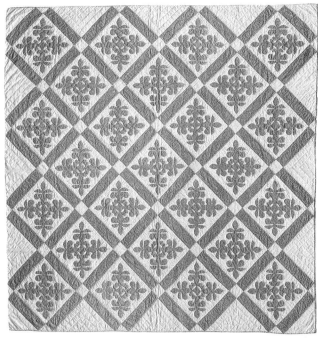

Sarah Beckner is a great-aunt of the current owners of her applique quilt *(left)*. They are descendants of the original Mennonite families who settled in the San Joaquin Valley of California.

Hettie Kulp Mininger made this fine applique quilt *(right)* when she was 19 years old. In 1962 she moved into her son Edward's home and gave the quilt to Edward and his wife.

Floral Applique (left)
82 x 95
Cotton
circa 1930
Reedley, California
Quiltmaker: Sarah Beckner
Owners: Arthur Eymann Bergthold
     and Patricia Ann Bergthold

Oak Leaf Applique (right)
78 x 78
Cotton
1893
Bucks County, Pennsylvania
Quiltmaker: Hettie Kulp Mininger
     (Mrs. J.D. Mininger)
Owner: Mrs. Edward P. Mininger

Oak Leaf Applique

68 x 85

Cotton

1878

McLean County, Illinois

Quiltmaker: Phoebe A. King Ernst

Owner: Hazel L. Straub Miller

Phoebe A. King carefully stitched her name and the date "1878" into the border of her quilt. Although she was only 19 years old, her applique work is impeccable. The swag border, done with five scallops on the lower edge, is smooth and balanced. Quilting is extremely generous and fine.

Phoebe was married in 1881. The quilt shows no wear and was apparently appreciated as a special quilt. Phoebe's granddaughter now treasures this memento of her grandmother, who died when Hazel was seven years old.

Catherine Haines was a Quaker woman, who ran a girls school where she taught stitchery. At age 35 she married Benjamin Miller and joined the Mennonite church. She and Benjamin had six children; she made quilts for each of them. Mary, the youngest daughter, received this quilt from her mother when she married in 1849. Catherine distributed patches to Mary's friends who appliqued them and signed their names. Some friends added short quotes on their patches.

Mary Miller Blessington handed the quilt to her daughter Mazie Blessington. Mazie never married. When Mazie died, this quilt was sold at public auction. Betty Herr, a great-granddaughter of the quiltmaker, bought the quilt.

Oak Leaf Friendship Quilt
72 x 84
Cotton
1849
Lancaster County, Pennsylvania
Quiltmaker: Catherine Haines Miller
Owner: M. Elizabeth Witmer Herr

Dresden Plate *(left)*
68 x 84
Cotton and wool
circa 1890
Champaign County, Illinois
Quiltmaker: Barbara Heiser Zehr
Owner: Margaret Oyer

Fan *(right)*
83 x 83
Wool
circa 1900
Rockingham County, Virginia
Quiltmaker: Sophia Showalter
Owner: Alice Blosser Trissel

Barbara Heiser Zehr was married to Bishop Peter Zehr, the organizer and first minister of East Bend Mennonite Church in Fisher, Illinois. Barbara pieced the quilt *(left)* and then carefully outlined each section with yellow feather stitching.

Margaret Oyer remembers seeing the quilt on the spare bed at her grandparents' house when she was a young girl.

Four fan patches come together to form a grid of circles on this quilt *(right)*. The single fan patches are nearly symmetrical, using alternating colors or symmetrical groupings of three colors. When they are joined in units of four, the color symmetry is broken. The overall effect is somewhat jumbled but interesting. A pieced border ties everything together.

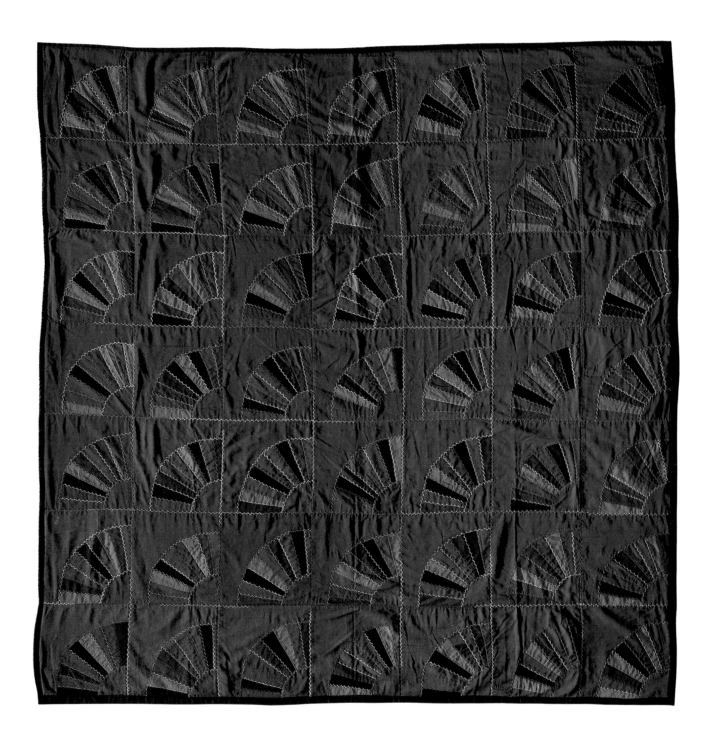

Mary Yoder hand-pieced each one of the 49 seven-inch fan blocks in this quilt. She then covered each seam with beautifully embroidered feather stitching in a variety of colors. The only machine stitching on the quilt was used to apply the binding.

Mary gave the quilt to her daughter Ida, who kept it till she was 85 years old. Ida then passed the quilt on to her niece Ruby because she shared her interest and involvement in quiltmaking.

Fan

75 x 75

Cotton

circa 1920

Johnson County, Iowa

Quiltmaker: Mary Yoder Yoder

Owner: Ruby Yoder Campos

Quiltmaker Priscilla Shantz Kolb shown in a wedding photo with her husband, Titus L. Kolb, in 1906.

Priscilla Shantz was known as a competent seamstress. She sewed not only for her mother and her sisters but also for neighbors and friends. She made her older sister Maggie's wedding dress, baby dresses for her little sister Susan, a traveling suit for her good friend Mabel Brown, and an assortment of other assignments from special to more ordinary garments. These ventures left her with a wide variety of fabric scraps which she saved for later use.

In 1902 Priscilla began work on this quilt for her hope chest. She arranged her scraps into large diamonds and put the diamonds together to form a large Crazy Patch Star quilt. Each seam is covered with elaborate embroidery in a host of different types of stitching. The quilt was finished in 1905.

Priscilla married Titus L. Kolb on November 28, 1906. After her marriage she restricted her sewing to the needs of her six growing children—five girls and one boy. Her daughter Myrtle remembers that the dresses her mother made were a bit more special than those of her friends'. Priscilla's years of sewing experience were displayed in her daughter's wardrobe.

The Crazy Star quilt was seldom used. However, Myrtle remembers that it was put on her bed when she was sick. Her mother would spread the Crazy Star over her, then, sitting beside her, she would point to the vaious patches, telling Myrtle stories about the different garments she had made. Thus the quilt provided comfort and warmth in many ways.

Myrtle was honored when her mother, several years before her death in 1985, said she wanted her to have the quilt.

Crazy Star
70 x 78
Cotton, wool, silk
1905
Waterloo County, Ontario, Canada
Quiltmaker: Priscilla Shantz Kolb
Owner: Myrtle Kolb Liechty

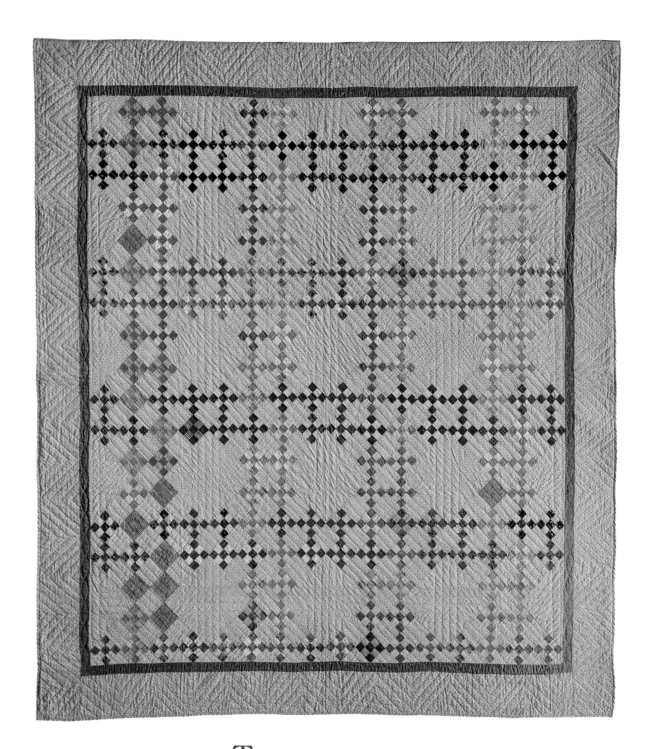

Nine-Patch

77 x 94

Cotton

circa 1910

Ohio

Quiltmaker: Catherine Mumaw

Owner: Ethel Mumaw

The patches that make up the nine-patch blocks on this quilt are precise one-inch squares. Though the quilt uses a variety of different fabrics (likely scraps from dresses, shirts and aprons), the squares are carefully grouped to form lines of similar colors across the surface of the quilt.

Catherine Mumaw was the wife of Amos Mumaw, a minister in Ohio. His ministerial responsibilities prompted them to move many times. Amos died in his fifties, leaving Catherine a widow.

This quilt, made by Catherine, now belongs to her granddaughter Ethel.

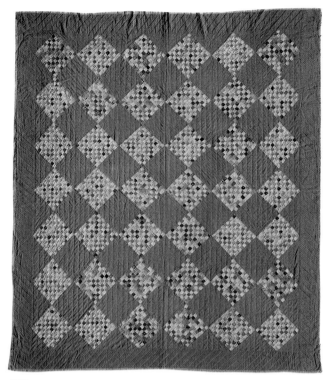

Barbara Amstutz Welty must have been an unusually patient and precise seamstress. This quilt *(left)* has 42 pieced blocks with 100 postage-stamp sized patches per block. Each pieced block is 6¾ inches square, and each tiny patch is smaller than ¾ inch square! Barbara began this quilt in 1900 and worked on it when her children were infants. She pieced and quilted the entire quilt by hand.

Because of its light weight, this quilt was used as a summer cover. After Mrs. Welty died, the quilt was passed to the current owner's aunt, who used it as a throw over her chair. When her aunt died, Carrie Miller bought the quilt at a private sale.

Carrie's grandmother, Barbara, always made her quilt tops from remnants of fabric, left after sewing clothes for her eight daughters and one son. She bought fabric only for the quilt backs.

Carrie's grandmother, aunts and mother made hundreds of quilts as gifts for missionaries. Today those quilts are scattered all over North America and in many places throughout the world.

Elizabeth Lehman started work on this quilt *(right)* as soon as she heard the news that her niece was expecting a baby. When John L. Horst, Jr. was born in 1938, his great-aunt Lizzie had his quilt finished. She had done the piecework (the small patches are each one-inch square) and then solicited the help of neighbors Annie and Susie Lehman to do the quilting.

Postage Stamp *(left)*
68 x 74
Cotton
circa 1905
Putnam County, Ohio
Quiltmaker: Barbara Amstutz Welty
Owner: Carrie J. Miller

Thirty-Six-Patch *(right)*
90 x 90
Cotton
1938
Franklin County, Pennsylvania
Quiltmakers: Pieced by Elizabeth
*   Hunsecker Lehman; quilted by*
*   Annie and Susie Lehman*
Owner: John L. Horst, Jr.

Nine-Patch *(left)*

69 x 75

Cotton

1876

Sterling, Illinois

Quiltmaker: Joseph S. Shoemaker

Owner: Karen Kreider Yoder

Double Nine-Patch *(right)*

79 x 79

Cotton

circa 1895

McPherson County, Kansas

Quiltmaker: Mary Bontrager Yoder

Owner: Joan Gerber

During the winter of 1876, Joseph Shoemaker cut his leg while working on the farm. The cut required that he spend the remainder of the winter inside. Joseph's mother put him to work piecing this Nine-Patch quilt top *(left)*.

The following year Joseph married Elizabeth Secrist Brubaker, who was an avid and excellent quilter. Joseph's quilt did not match hers in quality, so his was placed in a trunk and never used. The quilt was passed on to their daughter, Stella Shoemaker Kreider, who in turn gave it to her granddaughter.

Cotton dresses and aprons, no longer suitable for wearing, were a ready source of quilt scraps. A Nine-Patch quilt *(right)* incorporates these leftover fabric scraps handily. This example uses a multitude of prints. Many of the individual Nine-Patch blocks use four or five different fabrics within each square.

A simple but pleasing quilt, this Nine-Patch appears to have been made with fabric from the scrap bag. Its background and border are color coordinated, however. That fabric was likely purchased specifically for the quilt, because of the quantity needed for those parts.

Nine-Patch

86 x 86
Cotton
circa 1900
Lancaster County, Pennsylvania
Quiltmaker: Mrs. Jacob Miller
Owner: Martha Clark

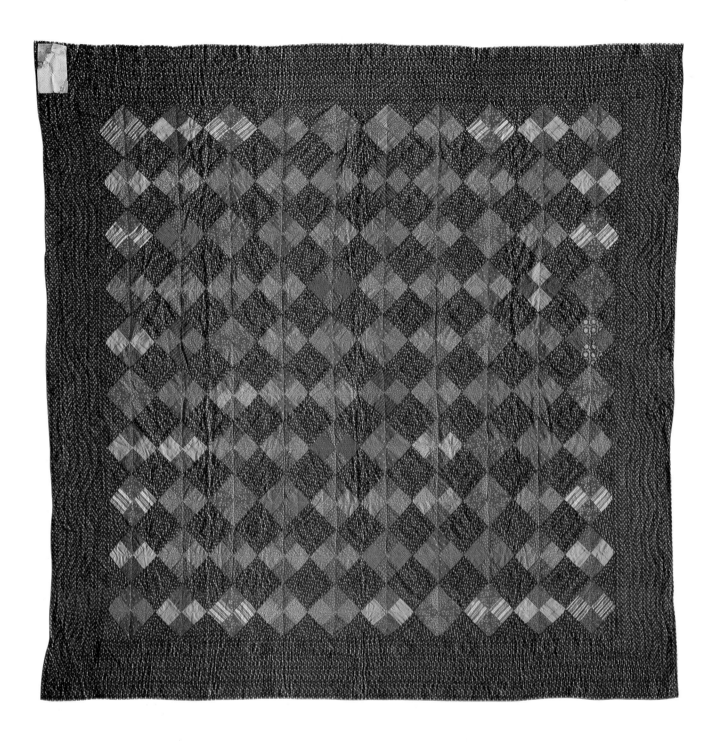

Four-Patch

79 x 79
Cotton
1909
Lancaster County, Pennsylvania
Quiltmaker: Fannie Rohrer Root
Owner: J. Clyde Root

A yellowed note pinned to the corner of this quilt reads: "From Grandmother Root to Clide Root 1909." The boy's name was actually "Clyde" but Grandma had not heard the name before and did not know how it was spelled. Clyde was born in 1901. His quilt was never used and remains in pristine condition. The Four-Patch blocks seem to be scrap fabrics but the background and border were likely purchased specifically for the quilt.

Dorcas Horst was born in 1903 and learned to sew at age six. This quilt represents her first effort at quiltmaking. Dorcas pieced the blocks by hand, and her mother stitched the blocks together with the sewing machine. The white triangles are cut from fabrics given as gifts to Dorcas when she was a baby to be made into dresses. But the dresses were never made, giving Dorcas the opportunity to use the fabrics in her first quilt.

Four-Patch in Blockwork

73 x 80
Cotton
circa 1909
Wakarusa, Elkhart County, Indiana
Quiltmaker: Dorcas Horst
Owner: Mennonite Historical Library,
Goshen, Indiana

Nine-Patch (left)
80 x 80
Cotton
circa 1910
Lancaster County, Pennsylvania
Quiltmaker: Barbara Brackbill
Owner: Verna M. Graham

Nine-Patch (right)
71 x 78
Cotton
circa 1884
Fulton County, Ohio
Quiltmaker: Elizabeth Conrad Frey
Owners: Lawrence and Marjora Miller

The practice of making a quilt for a namesake was quite common during the late 19th and early 20th centuries. This quilt *(left)* is an example of that custom. Barbara Brackbill made the quilt for her namesake granddaughter, Barbara (Brackbill) Graham.

The lines that were marked onto the fabric to indicate quilting patterns are still clearly visible, suggesting that this quilt *(right)* was never washed. When the quilt came up for sale at the public auction of his aunt Amanda's possessions, Lawrence and Marjora Miller bought it for $5.00. They believe the quilt was probably made for Lawrence's grandfather, Jacob Frey, by his mother, Elizabeth Conrad Frey.

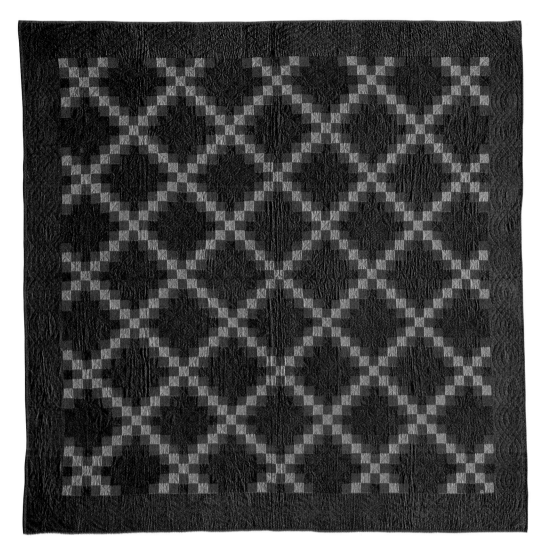

Barbara Hess Bomberger was born on Christmas day, 1829, a fact which seems reflected in the color choices she made in this Irish Chain. Barbara was not an avid quiltmaker, but she did make lovely pieces for each of her grandchildren. She made this one for her granddaughter, Barbara Snyder Charles, and presented it to her when she was 10 years old. Barbara wrote her name and the date on a piece of paper, and then sewed it to the back of the quilt where it remains to this day. Granddaughter Barbara never used the quilt because she didn't care for its dark colors. She loved quiltmaking and made many quilts herself.

Barbara lived on the farm where her grandparents had lived. When she moved off the farm, she gave the quilt to her daughter, Ethel Charles Buckwalter, who moved in. Ethel had an abundance of quilts from her mother, and she too never used the "Christmas" quilt. Ethel Charles Buckwalter passed the quilt to her daughter, Doris Buckwalter Nolt, when Ethel moved from the farmhouse and Doris moved in.

Thus, quilt, farm and family have remained together through the years. The quilt is now used as a decorative tablecover at Christmastime.

Irish Chain

78 x 79

Cotton

1897

Lancaster County, Pennsylvania

Quiltmaker: Barbara Hess Bomberger

Owner: Doris Buckwalter Nolt

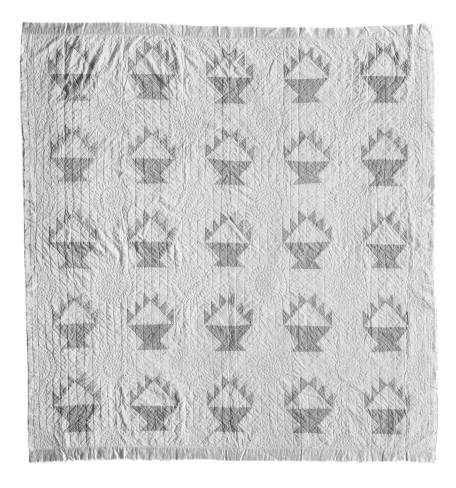

Basket
66 x 60
Cotton
1931
Marion County, Kansas
Quiltmaker: Frieda Ediger Barkman
Owner: Frieda Ediger Barkman

The story of the Basket quilt as written by its maker, Frieda Ediger Barkman.

In 1931 I finished the fourth grade. Mamma said, "Doing so well in school and having earned a spelling bee ribbon, you really are too old to just play all summer. You may be ready for a grown-up project."

I did wash dishes, hoe the garden, peel potatoes and help with the canning—so what did she have in mind?

"Would you like to make a quilt for your bed?"

"Oh yes, yes, yes!" I had sewed doll clothes since first grade.

My older brothers were skeptical. "Aw, she won't stay with it."

Mamma made quilts only from scraps during the Depression and Dust Bowl years, but for my quilt we shopped for unbleached muslin and (I could choose the color) solid pink cotton. In her sewing trunk we found lots of quilt patterns. Naturally I chose the most beautiful, intricate one, but Mamma wisely suggested a simple basket pattern—still with 20 pieces per block.

I cut till my thumb was calloused.

I sewed till I saw only pink and white day and night.

I began to weary. The Kansas summer was hot with no electric fans.

Papa carried the foot-propelled sewing machine outdoors. The shade of the cottonwood tree, the company of cats, a dog, chickens and two brothers gave me new impetus. The machine whirred; the block pile grew.

Mamma pressed the patches and readied them for quilting. Papa set the frame up in my bedroom. Here Mamma taught me to quilt and helped. Here we spent many good mother-daughter hours together.

The project caught my neighbor girlfriends' fancy, which resulted in a quilting party in my bedroom.

My brothers decided they too would quilt, which was a wordless way of acknowledging I would stick with the project to the end, and they wanted to help. But my demand for clean hands and small stitches thinned their enthusiasm and they soon decided they needed to help Papa in the field.

Summer neared September and I still quilted. When my eyes stung from the small stitches and my fingers bled from needle pricks, I paused, looked out my second story window.

A stream meandered through a meadow, white-faced cattle lazied under cottonwoods, and distant farmsteads dotted the horizon. My ten year old eyes saw more than cows and barns. In the peace of that pastoral scene my spirit awoke to the joy of work, the beauty of life and the omnipresence of God.

I returned to school in September with the satisfaction of achievement and a little more grown up, symbolized by the new quilt on my bed.

Quiltmaker Frieda Ediger Barkman is shown with other spelling bee contest winners in Marion County, Kansas. She made her Basket quilt the same year she won the blue ribbon in the spelling bee. Winners are (left row front to back) Alvin Dyck, Frieda Ediger Barkman, Frieda's brother Wilbur Ediger, (right row front to back) Kurt Dyck, Ruth Funk, Esther Voth.

Double Irish Chain

77 x 78

Cotton

circa 1880

Franklin County, Pennsylvania

Quiltmakers: Mattie Stauffer, her
mother and sisters

Owner: Thelma P. Plum

Mattie Stauffer was from a family of four sisters and two brothers. Only one of her sisters married, but each sibling had a chest full of quilts and comforters the family had made. The married sister was the last surviving member of the family, and she inherited the family estate. She divided the quilts and comforters among her grandchildren. Each granddaughter received a quilt and each grandson a comforter. Granddaughter Thelma P. Plum was the fortunate recipient of this one.

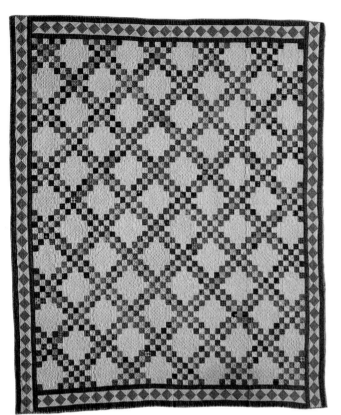 

Margaret Blosser (Aunt Maggie) remained single and lived at home with her parents until well into her middle age. She and her mother were able to spend many hours quilting together. Aunt Maggie became known as one of the finest quilters in the area.

The maker of this quilt *(left)* was a great-aunt to the present owner, who is her namesake.

Anna Showalter Trissel was widowed when her youngest son, David, was three years old. She died two years later, when David was five. Before her death, she made this quilt *(right)* for her young son.

David grew up and married Lily Hess. He died eight months later. Lily was remarried to David's brother, John Trissel, in 1910. They gave this quilt to their daughter Iva, the second of six children.

Irish Chain *(left)*
79 x 96
Cotton
circa 1880
Rockingham County, Virginia
Quiltmaker: Margaret Blosser Martin
Owner: Margaret Suter Brunk

Irish Chain *(right)*
75 x 85
Cotton
circa 1880
Rockingham County, Virginia
Quiltmaker: Anna Showalter Trissel
Owner: Iva M. Trissel

Double Irish Chain (left)
82 x 91
Cotton
circa 1930
Rockingham County, Virginia
Quiltmaker: Mary Hartman Heatwole
Owner: Mary Ethel Lahman
    Heatwole

Double Irish Chain with
Strawberry Applique (right)
82 x 63
Cotton
1880
McPherson County, Kansas
Quiltmaker: Katharine Schrag
    Wedel
Owner: Kauffman Museum, North
    Newton, Kansas

Mary Hartman married John E. Heatwole, a farmer who raised, and marketed by catalogue, a wide variety of thoroughbred poultry. The Heatwoles had three children.

Mary's quilting skills are apparent in the careful execution of this pattern *(left)*. The quilt was given to Mary Ethel, granddaughter of the quiltmaker, who was only two years old when her grandma died.

Family history credits Katharine Schrag with making this quilt *(right)* in 1880 when she was just 15 years old. The backing that wraps to the front to become the binding appears to be drapery fabric made in the 1930s. The quilting was done by machine, but most of the piecing and applique was done by hand. The family surmises that the less precise piecing and applique was also done with a machine, and that the back was added at a later date.

The work on this quilt is quite crude. Katharine was known as a more proficient flower gardener than quilter. Her love of flowers is displayed by the addition of nine patches of appliqued strawberries.

Even though it is undated, oral history acknowledges this to be the oldest known quilt to have been made by Russian Mennonite immigrants in Kansas.

Annie G. Herr Erb was the mother of 11 children—six boys and five girls. Her intention was to make seven quilts for each of her daughters. She was not able to meet her goal, but many of her quilts still survive in the family.

This quilt was made for daughter Emma Herr Erb Peifer. She passed the quilt on to her granddaughter, Joanne Ranck Dirks.

Double T

84 x 84

Cotton

circa 1915

Lancaster County, Pennsylvania

Quiltmaker: Annie G. Herr Erb

Owner: Joanne Ranck Dirks

Tulip or Carolina Lily

85 x 85
Cotton
circa 1875
Montgomery County, Pennsylvania
Quiltmaker: probably Maria Gehman
*   Ruth*
Owner: Mennonite Historians of
*   Eastern Pennsylvania,*
*   Harleysville, Pennsylvania*

Mennonite Historians of Eastern Pennsylvania acquired this quilt as a gift from Mary Ann Moyer Althouse. She was the daughter of John L. and Anna Mary Ruth Moyer. Anna Mary Ruth was the daughter of Noah P. and Maria Gehman Ruth of Line Lexington Mennonite congregation. It is thought that Maria Gehman Ruth was the maker of the quilt.

Barbara Swartzendruber began making quilts when her mother was pregnant with her eleventh (and last) child. Barbara's father required that she and her sister Mattie stay home from school on alternate weeks to help their mother. Barbara's memory is that she didn't learn much at school, but she got a lot of quiltmaking done for the family.

Carolina Lily

78 x 78

Cotton

circa 1925

Blaine County, Oklahoma

Quiltmaker: Barbara Swartzendruber

Privately owned

Carolina Lily
68 x 80
Cotton
1940
Mahoning County, Ohio
Quiltmaker: Anna Metzler
Owner: Alice Hill

Anna made this quilt for her granddaughter Kathryn Lehman Albrecht while she lived with Kathryn's family. Kathryn could not understand why her grandmother insisted on finishing a quilt when there were many preparations to be made for her wedding. Only later did she discover the quilt was to be her wedding gift. Kathryn has since passed the quilt on to her daughter.

During the winter of 1912 Henry Diller was housebound with Parkinson's disease. The family bought fabric, Henry pieced the quilt *(left)*, and his wife Amanda quilted it. They passed the quilt on to their son who handed it on to his daughter. She in turn gave the quilt to her daughter, a great-granddaughter of the quilt makers.

Hermina Haury's family remembers that she always had a quilt in the frame in the dining room for some member of the family. She was also an active member of the Bethel College Mennonite Church quilting group.

North Carolina Lily *(left)*
70 x 86
Cotton
1912
Allen County, Ohio
Quiltmakers: Henry and Amanda
      Diller
Owner: Sandra Miller

Carolina Lily *(right)*
79 x 99
Cotton
circa 1930
Harvey County, Kansas
Quiltmaker: Hermina Kraft Haury
Owner: Ada Mae Haury (Mrs. Robert
      Haury)

Flower Garden *(left)*
78 x 86
Cotton
circa 1930
Montgomery County, Pennsylvania
Quiltmaker: Clara Detweiler (Mrs.
John Detweiler)
Owner: Mrs. Esther Bergey

Esther Bergey's grandmother, Clara Detweiler (February 14, 1870—February 8, 1952), made many quilts, including one for each of her children. When she was about 60 years old, she made this one *(left)* for Esther's mother. As a child, Esther remembers going with her mother and grandmother to Allentown, Pennsylvania, to buy fabric for quilts. Her grandmother would take her Flower Garden template along so she could buy fabric with a pattern that suited the six-sided flower pieces.

When Esther's mother died, Esther became the heir to this beauty, which she has used only a few times.

Grandmother's Flower Garden
(right)
72 x 88
Cotton
circa 1920
Williams County, Ohio
Quiltmaker: Catherine Ricker
Stuckey
Owners: Lawrence and Marjora Miller

Catherine Ricker Stuckey made this quilt *(right)* for her daughter Malinda Stuckey Short in celebration of her marriage in 1919. She both pieced and quilted it by hand. Malinda's daughter Marjora purchased the quilt at a family sale following Malinda's death.

Sarah Diener Kennel (1852-1928) made this quilt as a wedding gift for her daughter, Kate Kennel Yost (1881-1980).

Flower Garden

76 x 85

Cotton

circa 1905

Lancaster County, Pennsylvania

Quiltmaker: Sarah Diener Kennel

Owner: Privately owned

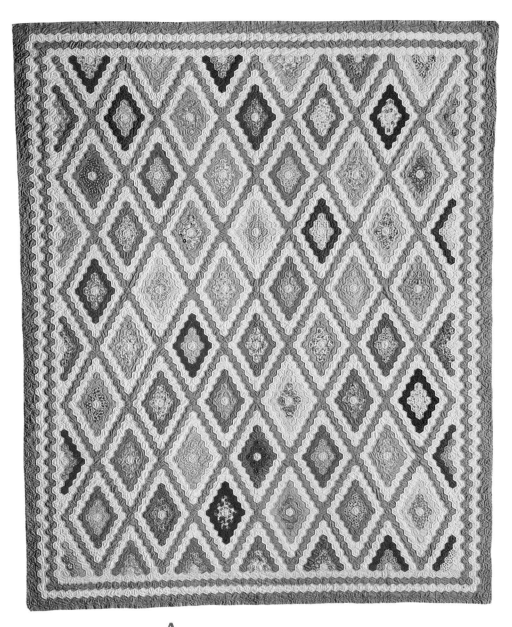

Field of Diamonds

76 x 92

Cotton

circa 1930

Turner County, South Dakota

Quiltmaker: Anna Preheim Graber

Owner: Florine Plenert

A woman who loved quiltmaking, Anna Preheim Graber made some one hundred quilts in her lifetime. She liked piecework more than quilting, so her practice was to piece the tops, and then invite her daughters for quilting bees to get the quilting done. That finished, Anna would take over again and do the binding.

Her granddaughters feel especially close to her quilts since she made many of them from scraps of fabric left from dresses their mothers had made for them.

Anna had a special knack for matching colors. She would choose a scrap of fabric and then send someone to the store with specific instructions to buy either solid colored fabric(s) exactly like the color in one or more sections of the scrap. By using differing solids with the same scrap, she highlighted a variety of colors. The same print looked different, depending upon the colors beside it in the quilt top.

The family referred to this quilt *(left)* as a "beggar's quilt" because it used so many different fabrics. Daughter Dorcas remembers the quilt being placed on her bed during an extended childhood illness, about 1915. She passed her long bedridden hours by examining the quilt to find two like patches. After hours of looking she recalls she finally discovered two made from the same fabric.

Before she was married, Mary moved from her family home in Juniata County, Pennsylvania, to Reading, Pennsylvania, for a job. She filled her long evenings with cutting and sewing tiny patches for this Flower Garden quilt *(right)*. (Mary still has the $.10 scissors she used to do the cutting.)

After the flowers were pieced, she was not sure how to put them all together. Her sister Iona helped her devise a plan to piece tiny green diamond-shaped pieces (1" x ½") between the groupings to form a path among the flowers. The quilt has never been used except for display when entertaining company.

Honeycomb *(left)*
66 x 77
Cotton
1895
Wakarusa, Elkhart County, Indiana
Quiltmaker: Anna Beutler
Owner: Mennonite Historical Library,
        Goshen, Indiana

Grandmother's Flower Garden
(right)
77 x 97
Cotton
1934
Berks County, Pennsylvania
Quiltmaker: Mary
        Shelley Hershey
Owner: Mary Shelley Hershey

Dresden Plate Variation
70 x 83
Cotton
circa 1905
Reedley, California
Quiltmaker: Sarah Beckner
Owners: Arthur Eymann Bergthold and Patricia Ann Bergthold

Art Bergthold married Mary Eymann in 1934. Each of their grandparents were the first of their families—and some of the first Mennonites—to settle in the San Joaquin Valley of California.

Mary's grandfather, Daniel T. Eymann, had owned and operated with his wife and family a successful farm on the plains of Kansas. But Daniel's bachelor brother had left the plains for the West Coast. On his visits back to the farm he spoke fondly of California's climate, beauty and opportunity. Having spent years withstanding the rigors of Kansas winters, Daniel and his wife Babetta decided to escape for a few weeks during the winter and visit this land of promise. They spent time in Upland because they knew a few people living there and were aware that the town had a small Mennonite congregation. Several visits and some years later, Daniel purchased land near Upland. In the autumn of 1903, the family moved to a new home in California.

During this time agents of the Sante Fe Railroad were actively working at drawing more people to settle in the West. Having known Daniel as a Kansas farmer, one of the agents convinced him to consider buying land near Reedley in the San Joaquin Valley. Daniel and his oldest son August scouted the area and found it very promising. The land was less expensive than in Upland, and a move there would allow the family to expand, yet stay together as sons and daughters married. Six months after they moved to Upland, the family relocated to the Valley. The Eymanns were the first Mennonites to settle in this area.

They eventually built five houses for family members in close proximity to each other, referred to by the neighbors as Eymann Colony.

Finding it a desirable place to live and wanting to establish a Mennonite church there, Daniel began inviting other Mennonites from the Midwest and the East to consider the move. His endeavors were quite successful. One of the early families recruited was the Jacob Bergtholds (Art's grand-parents) who moved from Minnesota in 1904.

As more families arrived, a missionary society and quilting circle were begun for women. While they quilted in the parlor, two mothers watched an Eymann baby girl and a Bergthold baby boy playing on the floor. Each is said to have commented, "Wouldn't it be something if they grew up and married." Grown baby Art Bergthold and grown baby Mary Eymann married in 1934. A year later their son Arthur Eymann Bergthold was born.

The younger Arthur's job required that he and his family move from the San Joaquin Valley. But 22 years ago, his last transfer allowed them to move back home. They bought the August Eymann house where Arthur's mother, Mary Eymann Bergthold, was born and raised. Then Arthur's parents bought the Dan Eymann house next door when Mrs. Eymann (Lelia) moved to a nursing home. Lelia left her quilts in the house, and Art's parents, knowing that Pat and Art cherish family heirlooms, passed the quilts from Art's great-aunt on to them. This quilt was made for Lelia Eymann by her mother, Sarah Beckner.

This photo (top) shows the quilters of the First Mennonite Church's women's society started by Mary Eymann. Mary is seated center front holding her daughter Mary, who later married Arthur Bergthold. Their son Arthur and his wife Pat are currently the owners of the quilt.

The First Mennonite Church (bottom), founded by the Eymanns, is shown shortly after being constructed in 1906.

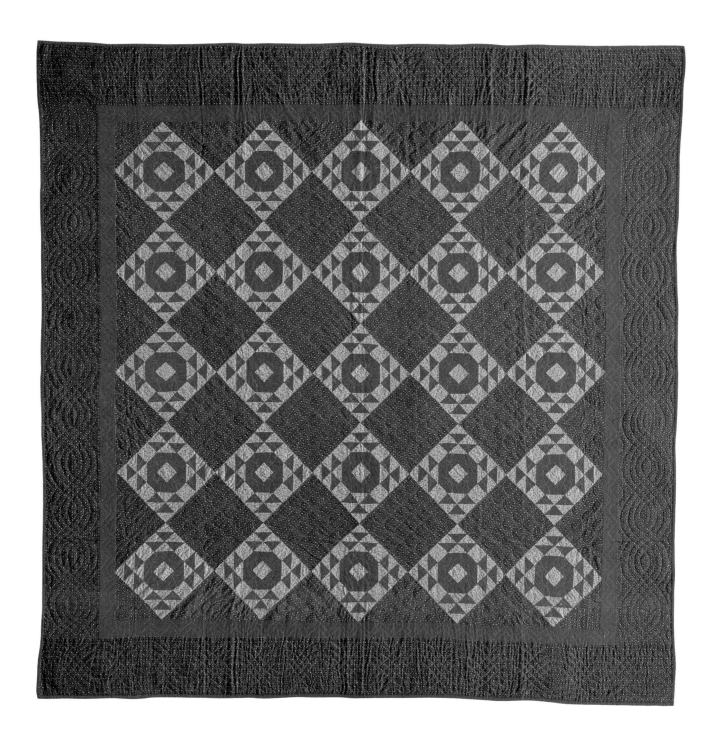

Crown of Thorns

81 x 82
Cotton
circa 1890
Lancaster County, Pennsylvania
Quiltmaker: Unknown
Owner: Joann Metzler Herr

Though no one is sure who made this quilt, it is known that it was made for Susan B. Bucher. Susan never married and never used the quilt. When she moved to California, she sold her quilt to her sister, Anna Bucher Kready. Anna passed the quilt on to Mary Kready Metzler, who later passed it to Joanne Metzler Herr. It has remained unused through the generations.

Ella Kurtz Kopp was born in 1892 near Ephrata, Pennsylvania. It is believed that this quilt was made for Ella by someone in her family. Its condition indicates that Ella likely never used it. She passed the quilt on to her son.

Crown of Thorns

90 x 90

Cotton

circa 1910

Lancaster County, Pennsylvania

Quiltmaker: Unknown

Owners: Nel and LaMar Kopp

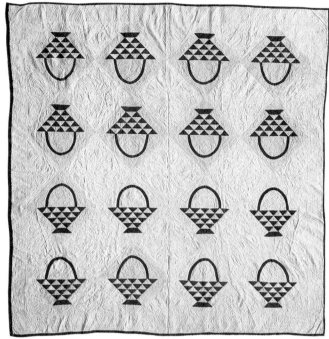

Baskets *(left)*
64 x 74
Cotton
circa 1900
Allen County, Ohio
Quiltmaker: Marianne Zingg
Badertscher
Owner: Marty Hostetler

Baskets *(right)*
84 x 84
Cotton
circa 1870
Fairview County, Michigan
Quiltmaker: Nancy Hertzler Hartzler
Owner: Mildred Miller

Marianne Zingg Badertscher (1855-1934) left Switzerland in the early 1870s and, with her husband Frederick, eventually settled in western Ohio by way of Wayne County, Ohio.

This quilt *(left)* now belongs to Marianne's granddaughter, who carries on the tradition of quiltmaking.

Nancy Hertzler Hartzler (1831-1872) pieced this quilt *(right)* by hand, appliqued the basket handles by hand, quilted it by hand and bound it by hand! Nancy made this quilt for her daughter Elizabeth Hartzler Miller. Elizabeth and her daughter Maude Miller Bergey also made many quilts, but they usually employed a sewing machine for piecing and binding.

This quilt was made by the current owner's great-grandmother and was given to Mildred by her grandmother around 1940.

Sometimes beautiful quilts are made, put into chests, and passed from generation to generation without much notice. This one remains in its family of origin (it was purchased at a public auction of a great-aunt's possessions), but the details of who made it, when, and for what occasion have been lost.

Baskets

95 x 95

Cotton

circa 1900

Lancaster County, Pennsylvania

Quiltmaker: Unknown

Privately owned

Flying Geese

82 x 89
Cotton
circa 1865
Lancaster County, Pennsylvania
Quiltmaker: Lizzie Graver
Privately owned

Lizzie Graver displayed true daring in the design and assembly of this quilt. The acute angles of the pattern are enhanced by the bold complementary colors of the fabrics. A floral quilting motif flows through the border, and quilted flowers are inserted in the 90 green quadrangles of the quilt's interior.

This simple piecework *(left)* is quilted with cable and feather designs in alternate bars. The two bars at each side break the rhythm with zigzag quilting. Solid red and green fabrics were frequently combined in a variety of patterns by quiltmakers of this era. The complementary colors bring energy and warmth when used side by side.

Though it is not certain who made this quilt, it was passed to Betty from her father's side of the family. It is presumed that her grandmother Elizabeth made the quilt.

The owner of this quilt remembers that this quilt *(right)* was used—but only rarely. Though she is not sure who made the quilt, she knows it came from her father—Chester D. Ranck—and his side of the family. Although the pieced pattern is quite simple, each color is quilted with a different vertical quilting pattern.

Bars *(left)*
81 x 85
Cotton
circa 1900
Lancaster County, Pennsylvania
Quiltmaker: probably Elizabeth Neff
Owners: Richard and Betty Neff
*   Pellman*

Rainbow *(right)*
70 x 80
Cotton
circa 1900
Lancaster County, Pennsylvania
Quiltmaker: Uncertain
Owner: Evelyn M. Becker

Album Patch

84 x 88
Cotton
1885
Lancaster County, Pennsylvania
Quiltmakers: Friends of Rebecca Miller Reesor
Owner: Ruth Wideman Reesor

Christian Reesor is a descendant of Peter Risser who moved from Elizabethtown, Pennsylvania to Canada in 1804. The name changed from Risser to Reesor sometime during that transition.

As a Mennonite bishop, Christian visited many churches and attended church conferences in the States. His ancestral connections and relatives drew him especially to Pennsylvania.

Christian married Adelaine Grove and they had a family of three daughters and one son. When the oldest was 11 and the youngest two years old, Adelaine died, leaving Christian to raise the children alone. With help and support from family and friends he was able to continue his church work and travels.

During one of his visits to Pennsylvania, Christian noticed a woman who was working at the home of his friends. However, he found no opportunity to meet or talk with her. When it was time to leave, Christian deliberately left his hat there, providing a reason to return to the home. On his next visit he met and talked with Rebecca Miller. Their initial meeting began a relationship carried on through the mail. This correspondence was complicated by the fact that Rebecca could neither read nor write. The woman she worked for read Christian's letters aloud to Rebecca and then wrote Rebecca's dictated reply. Christian and Rebecca corresponded from 1881 until 1885. They were married at the bride's home in Pennsylvania in 1885. Rebecca was 47 and Christian 56 years old.

Christian's two older daughters were married just prior to him in

This house, built in 1878 by Christian Reesor of York County, Ontario, Canada, is the place Rebecca Miller came to as a bride in 1885.

1884 and 1885. The family surmised that Christian delayed his marriage until his daughters were wed. Rebecca was welcomed warmly by Christian's family and was know affectionately as "Grandma Becky."

This quilt traveled with Rebecca by train to her new home in Canada. It consists of 25 blocks, each with a name written in the same careful script in the center of each patch. It is not clear whether the quilt was made while Rebecca was a teenager, or whether it was a tribute to her prior to her marriage and subsequent move from her home area.

The quilt was passed from Rebecca and Christian to Christian's son, Thomas. Thomas gave the quilt to his daughter, Elizabeth Reesor Wideman, who in turn gave it to her daughter, Ruth.

Rebecca, a quilter herself, made quilts for each of her grandchildren after she was married.

Ocean Waves

75 x 75

Cotton

circa 1930

Lancaster County, Pennsylvania

Quiltmaker: Lizzie Stoner

Owner: Helen Shenk Good

Lizzie Stoner made this quilt as a wedding gift for Henry and Margaret Shenk, who were married November 12, 1930. Because he was the oldest sibling in his family, Henry was the beneficiary of his Aunt Lizzie's practice of giving gifts to her nieces' and nephews' eldest children.

This quilt was seldom used, except on guest beds or on Sundays when company came. Henry and Margaret Shenk passed the quilt on to their daughter Helen.

The Ocean Waves pattern easily accommodates a large variety of scrap fabrics. Here the pieces are arranged with light and dark triangles opposite each other. This creates an undulating rhythm over the whole quilt top. The triangles that comprise the sawtooth inner border are just slightly larger than the triangles in the Ocean Wave pattern.

Though it is not known for certain, Becky Longenecker believes the quilt was made for her mother Kathryn prior to her marriage to Phares Longenecker in 1915.

Ocean Waves

81x 81
Cotton
circa 1910
Lancaster County, Pennsylvania
Quiltmaker: Unknown
Owner: Becky Longenecker

Shoofly *(left)*

71 x 82

Cotton

1903

McPherson County, Kansas

Quiltmaker: Anna Bitikofer Selzer

Owner: Berta I. Miller

This quilt *(left)* was made by Berta Miller's grandmother, Anna Bitikofer Selzer, who was born in Holmes County, Ohio, on January 10, 1857. She married Henry Selzer on November 27, 1879. Their son—the owner's father—was born upstairs in their log cabin home near Dundee, Ohio, on July 20, 1880. In 1884 the family moved to McPherson County, Kansas, settling near Canton, Kansas, in the Spring Valley community.

The owner's parents, Alvin Selzer and Nora Lauchs, were married on September 20, 1903 in Nora's home. This quilt was a wedding gift for Alvin and Nora.

Tumbling Blocks *(right)*

80 x 94

Cotton

circa 1870

Lancaster County, Pennsylvania

Quiltmaker: Mary Ann Herr Witmer

Owner: Susan Herr Burkholder

Mary Ann Herr Witmer made this quilt *(right)* for the hired man's bed. She used scraps from aprons and dresses—"nothing too fancy." The quilt was also used on her son's bed.

Mary Ann eventually gave the quilt to her daughter, who passed it to her daughter Susan (the current owner), when she needed more covers for the beds of her five children. As a child, Susan was fascinated with trying to see the tumbling blocks and/or stars in the pattern. Despite its years of use, the quilt remains in good condition.

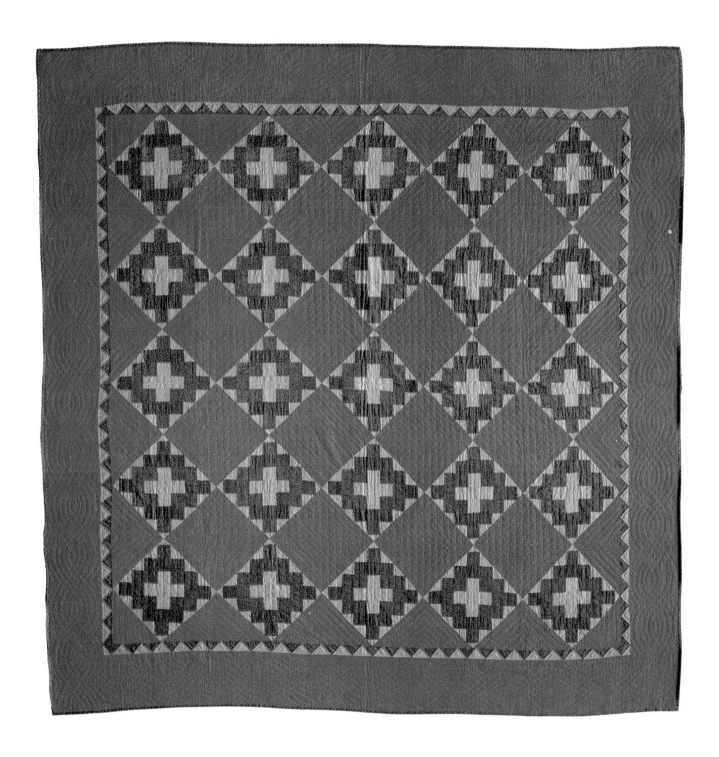

The family believes this quilt was a wedding gift for Harvey E. Metzler, who was married on October 22, 1908. Harvey's mother, Lizzie, quilted the initials "HEM" in a corner of the quilt.

This quilt appears to have spent most of its life in a chest. Debra Shank Miller, a great-granddaughter of Lizzie's, remembers the special occasions as a child when her mother (a daughter of Harvey's) showed her treasures from her chest, especially this quilt.

Album

84 x 84

Cotton

circa 1908

Lancaster County, Pennsylvania

*Quiltmaker: Elizabeth (Lizzie) Erb
    Metzler*

Owner: Debra Shank Miller

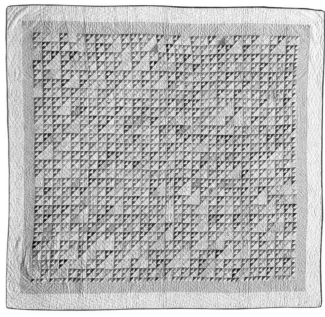

Sunburst *(left)*

71 x 76

Cotton

circa 1915

Ontario, Canada

Quiltmaker: Rebecca Miller Reesor

Owner: Anna Holmes

Triangles *(right)*

69 x 73

Cotton

circa 1910

Franklin County, Pennsylvania

Quiltmaker: Lydia Hunsecker
      Lehman Horst

Owner: John L. Horst, Jr.

Rebecca Miller of Pennsylvania married Christian Reesor of Ontario in 1885 and moved with him to Canada. There she pieced this quilt *(left)* for her step-daughter Elizabeth, prior to her marriage in 1919. The quilt was used only on the spare bed when guests and relatives from the United States came to visit and spend the night. The quilt has been passed from Elizabeth Reesor Wideman to her daughter Anna.

A masterpiece of tedious handwork, this quilt, with its 4280 triangles, plus border, was pieced entirely by hand. Along two sides (at right angles to each other) lies an inner border of continuous small triangles which alternate light and dark fabrics. This creates a sawtooth border along two sides, although the pattern is almost lost in the maze of triangles throughout the quilt. There is no explanation about why the sawtooth design was not continued along the other two sides. Perhaps the quiltmaker believed the sawtooth would conflict on those sides with the blocks that consist of four pieced triangles the same size as the sawtooth.

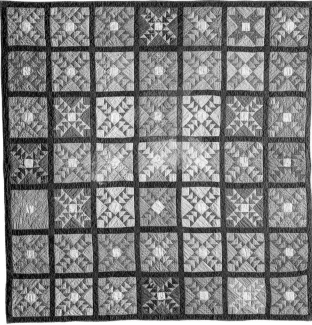

Susannah's careful planning of this quilt resulted in alternating and overlapping negative and positive circles.

Susannah was born in Goshen, Indiana, October 5, 1856. She married John Henry Loucks on January 23, 1879. Together they moved by train to Peabody, Kansas, in July of 1879. They settled in McPherson County, beginning their farming operation using a team of oxen.

Before Susannah died at 88 years of age, she had made quilts for each of her 35 grandchildren. This was Florence Selzer Schulty's, who, just before her death, gave it to her sister, Berta Miller.

World Without End (left)
76 x 84
Cotton
circa 1925
McPherson County, Kansas
Quiltmaker: Susannah Smith Loucks
Owner: Berta I. Miller

The center block of this quilt *(right)* says "property of William Gross." The remaining 48 patches contain names of William's friends. The quilt was made by his friends and presented to him on the occasion of his marriage. The quilt has been handed down through the generations, the most recent transfer being to the great-granddaughter of William Gross when she married in 1958.

The quilt survived a fire, although it was waterstained as a result.

Friendship Quilt (right)
90 x 90
Cotton
circa 1860
Bucks County, Pennsylvania
Quiltmakers: Friends of William
    Gross
Owner: Lorraine Gross Stutzman
    Myers

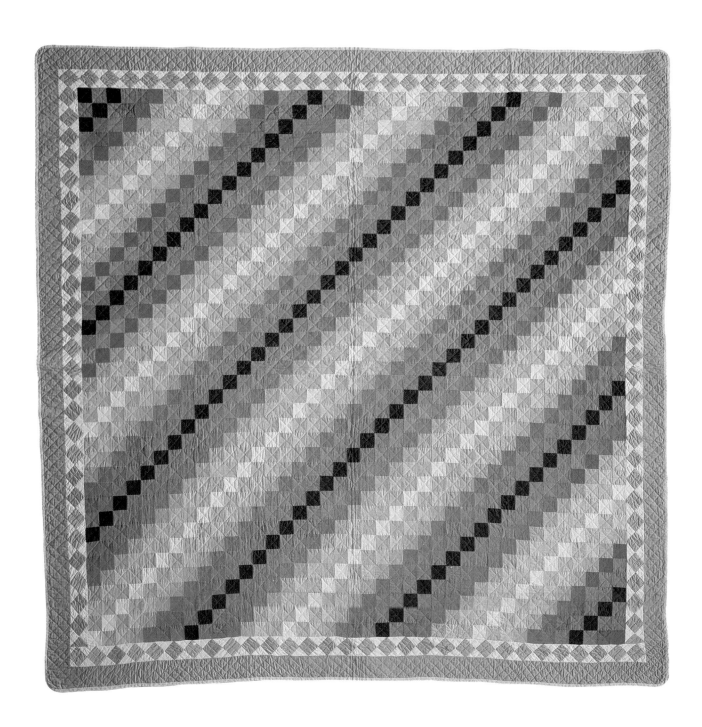

Sunshine and Shadow

85 x 85

Cotton

1941

Champaign County, Ohio

Quiltmaker: Priscilla Umble Allgyer

     (Mrs. S.E. Allgyer)

Owner: Olive Yoder

Priscilla Allgyer presented this quilt to her granddaughter Olive Yoder as a wedding gift and told her, "So your life will be! You will know both sunshine and shadow." Olive had already experienced some of life's shadow. Her mother died after a two-year illness, just before Olive's twentieth birthday, leaving her father, Olive and three younger children. The quilt made by her grandmother is, in Olive's words, "very special to me because I loved Grandma so much."

Susan Metzler Hottenstein and her husband Jacob were kept busy with the responsibilities of their young family and farm during the late 1800s. Susan had little time for quiltmaking.

That changed in 1909 when Susan and Jacob retired from the farm and moved into the town of East Petersburg. Susan became a prolific quiltmaker; her work was noted by her friends as being fine and neat.

She made this Monkey Wrench quilt *(left)*, along with a Lone Star and an Ocean Waves, for her grandson, Wayne B. Hottenstein. Wayne and Vera Hottenstein have kept the Ocean Waves, but passed the Monkey Wrench and Lone Star quilts to their sons John and Joe.

The Weaver family became the owners of this quilt when it was sold at public auction.

Monkey Wrench *(left)*
78 x 78
Cotton
circa 1910
Lancaster County, Pennsylvania
Quiltmaker: Susan Metzler
*   Hottenstein*
Owners: John and Carol Hottenstein

Double Wedding Ring (right)
61 x 74
Cotton
circa 1930
Rockingham County, Virginia
Quiltmaker: Rebecca Heatwole
Owners: Richard and Virginia
*   Weaver*

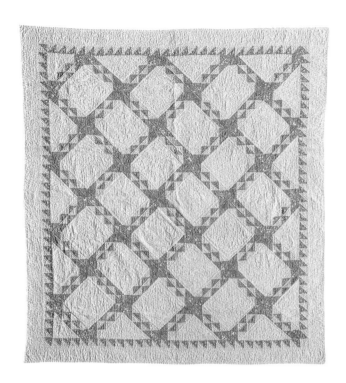 

Corn and Beans *(left)*
72 x 78
Cotton
1943
Elkhart County, Indiana
Quiltmakers: Pieced by Elizabeth
  Yoder; quilted by Nettie Short of
  Lucas County, Ohio
Owner: Martha Yoder Miller

In the year 1941, Elizabeth and Eli Yoder retired to live with their son and his family. During that time, Elizabeth spent hours at her treadle sewing machine, piecing quilts for her grandchildren. In fact, her eyesight improved through those years so that she no longer needed her eyeglasses!

When her granddaughter Martha (with whose parents Eli and Elizabeth lived) came home for a visit in June of 1947, Grandma Elizabeth told her, "Martha, this is the last time I'll see you." Martha assured her grandmother that she would return for a visit the next summer. But Elizabeth died the following December before they had the opportunity for another visit. This quilt *(left)*, made by her grandmother, holds many memories for Martha.

Path in the Sand *(right)*
79 x 82
Cotton
circa 1935
Waterloo County, Ontario, Canada
Quiltmaker: Annie Horst Bauman
Owner: Esther Brubacher Nafziger

This Path in the Sand *(right)* was one of eight quilts (plus comforters) made by Annie Horst Bauman for her daughter Leah in preparation for her marriage. She wanted her daughter to have "plenty of bedding."

Although as a member of the Old Order Mennonite church, Annie did not wear bright colors, her love for them is exhibited in her quiltmaking.

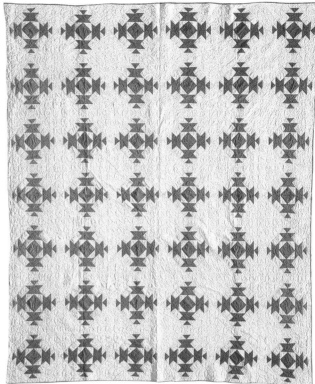

When Barbara Ebersole left her home in Centerville, Pennsylvania, in 1910 to work in the nearby city of Lancaster, her mother sent several well-worn family quilts with her. Barbara never used this quilt *(left)*, but put it into a cedar chest when she married Jacob E. Brubaker in 1918. Wool blankets were more in vogue at the time, and Barbara preferred them to her old quilt. The quilt now belongs to Barbara's daughter Naomi.

This quilt *(right)* was both hand-pieced and hand-quilted. Although it was used, it remains in good condition. Jacobina and Phoebe were great-grandmother and grandmother to the quilt's current owner.

Square in a Square *(left)*
73 x 76
Cotton
circa 1900
Lancaster County, Pennsylvania
Quiltmaker: Martha Stauffer
Ebersole (Mrs. Seth Ebersole)
Owner: Naomi E. Fast

Dove in the Window *(right)*
78 x 90
Cotton
circa 1900
Bureau County, Illinois
Quiltmakers: Jacobina Eigsti Sears
and her daughter Phoebe Sears
Culp
Owner: Nelda Buller

Crazy
68 x 73
Cotton, wool, silk
1909
Logan and Champaign counties, Ohio
Quiltmakers: Friends of Naomi Kauffman
Owner: Mary Vaughn Warye

In 1908, Christ Kauffman made an excursion from Logan County, Ohio, to Happy, Texas, where he had been told by friends he would find good land and happy days. There were already Mennonite families in Happy, and Christ purchased land and proceeded with plans for his family to relocate. The following year, much against the wishes of his wife and children (18-year-old Naomi and her three younger brothers), they all moved to Happy by train. The family rode in a passenger car while the livestock, farm implements and household goods followed in a freight car. They arrived in Texas in March of 1909.

They lived the first few weeks with another family until their own home could be built. Springtime in Texas was pleasant and balmy, but it could not cure the severe case of homesickness that Mrs. Kauffman suffered. June and July brought severe drought and the family was unable to raise any crops. By August they were discouraged and frustrated, so they loaded all their belongings on the train and headed back home to Ohio.

This Crazy quilt was made by Naomi's church friends before she left for Texas. Each of them made one of the blocks, autographed it and presented it to her. Naomi put the quilt together as she prepared to move with her family to Texas. There are 36 blocks in the quilt. In addition the top edge has six half-blocks.

Naomi never married. She raised ducks to sell after her family returned to Ohio. Later she kept busy by taking in washing for other people. She also became an avid quilter.

Naomi Kauffman, for whom the Friendship Crazy quilt was made, is shown here in her youth.

In October of 1981, Naomi, then an elderly woman, fell and broke her hip while trying to train a new kitten to stay in the basement overnight. Before retiring for the night she went to check on the kitten, fell over a newspaper barricade she had built, and broke her hip. Unable to get up, she laid there all night. Her cousin Mary, out for a morning walk, stopped by to check on Naomi and found her lying in the basement. Following her hospital stay, Mary cared for Naomi until she was strong enough to be alone.

When her heart weakened a year later, Naomi moved to a nursing home. From there, she called her cousin Mary and asked her to take the Crazy quilt from a chest in the attic and accept it as a gift. It was a cherished heirloom, twice given in friendship—once, to a young girl leaving for an unknown world, and then again to an old friend who had offered rescue and care.

All-Quilted *(left)*

77 x 87

Cotton

circa 1930

Rockingham County, Virginia

Quiltmaker: Lydia Lehman Shank

Owner: Margaret Shenk

All-White *(right)*

82 x 84

Cotton

1942

Lancaster County, Pennsylvania

Quiltmaker: Emma B. Snyder

Owner: Ann H. Landis

Lydia Lehman Shank made a whole-cloth quilt *(left)* for each of her eight children. Each lavishly stitched quilt was done in the same quilting design but of a different colored fabric.

Ann's grandmother, Emma B. Snyder, made this quilt *(right)* especially for her hope chest. Ann was to put it away and keep it until she had a home of her own. Emma lived to see that transpire.

Emma made quilts for each of her 34 grandchildren.

Della Krehbiel of Elyria, Kansas, became engaged to Herbert Flickinger of Moundridge, Kansas, in December of 1939. In February, while browsing a copy of *Country Gentleman* magazine, she noticed an illustration of the Floral Bouquet quilt. The pattern was available for 60 cents. Rather than spend the money for the pattern, Della drafted the design of one-inch squares herself. She pieced the quilt that winter and quilted it with the help of her aunts. She married Herb on July 3, 1941. The quilt was used on their bed only when guests were in their home.

In the spring of 1990, when Della's quilt was 50 years old, she proposed to the quilters of First Mennonite Church, McPherson, Kansas, that they duplicate it as their offering to the Mennonite Central Committee (MCC) auction for relief aid. They agreed and Della again drafted the design—this time for a queen-size quilt. Upon completion of the quilt, Della used the extra fabric to make a matching wallhanging and stuffed rabbit. Herb made a wall rack to accommodate the pieces for display. All the items were sold at the MCC sale in April of 1991.

Floral Bouquet

75 x 90
Cotton
1940
McPherson, Kansas
Quiltmaker: Della Flickinger
Owner: Della Flickinger

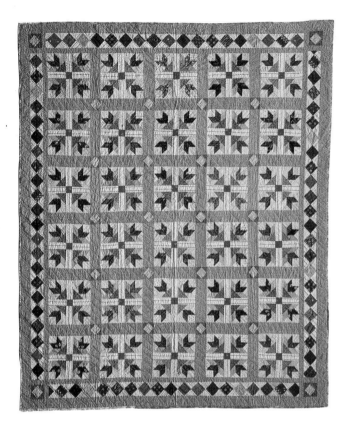

Goose Tracks *(left)*
72 x 89
Cotton
1918
Augusta County, Virginia
Quiltmaker: Bertha V. Martin
Owner: Mary E. Martin

Spider Web *(right)*
80 x 80
Cotton
circa 1938
Montgomery County, Pennsylvania
Quiltmaker: Clara Detweiler (Mrs.
*   John Detweiler)*
Owner: Mrs. Esther Bergey

This quilt *(left)* appears to be a scrap quilt utilizing a variety of prints in each Goose Tracks patch. Consistent use of red in the center of each patch, and uniform use of pink for the sashing and border, give the quilt an overall unity. Bertha made the quilt in 1918; her initials, "B.V.M.," and the year are embroidered along the one side.

Clara Detweiler had a cupboard in her sewing room where she kept fabrics. She likely drew from that storehouse when she made this quilt *(right)* as a wedding gift for her granddaughter, Esther, prior to her marriage to Curtis Bergey on April 16, 1938.

Clara and her husband John worked together at quiltmaking—John cut patches and marked the quilting designs; Clara wielded the needle and thread.

This Spider Web is constructed in strips sewn together to form pyramids. Clara used red in the same position in each pyramid so that when they were joined, each block had a red octagon close to its center.

Esther Hoover Groff was a farm girl who loved the outdoors. She preferred fieldwork to housework. After she and Noah H. Gross married, the couple moved to Ardmore so Noah could learn automotive repair. Esther did not like city living and appears to have developed emotional problems while living in the Philadelphia suburb. By 1927 her condition necessitated her admission to Harrisburg State Hospital. At that time, occupational therapy was unheard of and the family was responsible for providing something for the patient to do. Esther's mother and aunt supplied the materials for this quilt top *(left)* which she completed in the hospital. The top was never quilted, but a border was added so the top could be used as a spread.

Martha Schneider and Katherine Harder were good friends. They decided to make two identical quilts *(right)* together so each could have one. Their daughters Lovella and Lois both developed scarlet fever at the same time. Martha and Katherine saw this as an apt opportunity to finish their quilts. Martha and Lovella moved to the Harders' home and Menno Harder and two sons moved to the Schneiders' home. The scarlet fever ended, two quilts were completed, and the families returned to their own homes once again.

Floral Lattice Embroidery (left)
69 x 84
Cotton
circa 1927
Dauphin County, Pennsylvania
Quiltmaker: Esther Hoover Groff
Privately owned

New York Beauty (right)
81 x 88
Cotton
circa 1930
Reno County, Kansas
Quiltmakers: Martha Schneider (Mrs. Sam Schneider) and Katherine Harder (Mrs. Menno S. Harder)
Owner: Lovella Schneider Goering (Mrs. Joe W. Goering)

Who Are the Mennonites?

Mennonites have struggled for nearly five centuries with how to live in the world without being "worldly." Not only have they traditionally lived somewhat separate from the rest of society, they have attempted to take Jesus' Sermon on the Mount seriously—living as lights or, to parallel other biblical passages, living as yeast in a lump of dough or as salt in an unseasoned dish.

The "success" of their efforts to have their faith demonstrated in their lives is probably as varied as the number of persons who have ascribed to Mennonite beliefs. Some have lived consistently with their beliefs; others have fallen far short of their own ideals, as well as the biblical ideals they seek to follow.

How does one live on earth while following the directives of a heavenly kingdom? Is it enough to be concerned only for one's own spiritual health? Only for one's family? What about one's local and global neighbors? These questions have persisted for generations. They are still daily concerns for Mennonite scattered around the world.

The beginnings of the Mennonite church were in the early 1500s, during the Protestant Reformation which swept northern and central Europe. Originally known as "Anabaptists," the scattered group wanted a radical return to the teachings and practices of the New Testament. They felt that the emerging Protestant leaders were compromised in the reforms they were seeking, that they were settling for too little change. These more radical "Anabaptist" reformers sought *complete* separation of church and state and urged following Christ in *all* of daily life.

Basic understandings of Christian faith have characterized Mennonites since then, along with a series of distinguishing beliefs: voluntary adult baptism, living a commitment to peace, refusing the use of force and aggression, and living as full-time disciples of Jesus with an attitude of service toward all people.

While among the various groups of Mennonites there has been unity on these most fundamental issues of faith, there has been considerable variety in the ways those beliefs are expressed in daily living. Some Mennonites believe they can have the greatest positive effect on the society around them by following Christ in specific, identifiable ways. Traditionally their practices have stood in contrast to the prevailing society's. They have looked to their faith community for support and discipline, regarding themselves more as members of a "heavenly kingdom" than an "earthly" nation. Membership in the church is a serious commitment and is reserved for those who make a personal confession of faith and then live that faith, usually with an attitude of being separate from the world.

In more recent years, a growing number of Mennonites have opted for increasing involvement in the larger world. They have tried to effect change in their communities through participating in major businesses, entering academia, exerting political influence. Some have been able to do this while sustaining their commitment to Christ and the church community, while others have found it considerably more difficult to be active in both worlds.

Between these two poles—separation *from* the world, and active involvement *in* the world—have been many faithful Mennonites, some leaning in one direction, some leaning in the other. Mission activity has brought many persons to the Mennonite church whose heritages are not the northern European identities of the early Anabaptists. The result is a plethora of pluralism.

Today, Mennonites from over sixty countries around the world blend to form a diverse church. While their cultures, traditions and ethnic backgrounds are quite varied, their quest for faithfulness is remarkably uniform. In the absence of a written and codified theology, Mennonites have always had to search for how to express their beliefs in their lives. In that way, being a Mennonite is a process. How to apply the biblical text and the words of Jesus to one's life—in whatever era, setting or circumstance—is still the shaping force for these people, who seek to be salt, yeast and light in the world.

Readings & Sources

About Quilts

Bishop, Robert and Elizabeth Safanda. **A Gallery of Amish Quilts.** New York: E.P. Dutton, Inc., 1976.

Granick, Eve Wheatcraft. **The Amish Quilt.** Intercourse, PA: Good Books, 1989.

Haders, Phyllis. **Sunshine and Shadow: The Amish and Their Quilts.** New York: Universe Books, 1976.

Holstein, Jonathan. **The Pieced Quilt: An American Design Tradition.** Boston: New York Graphic Society, 1973.

Horton, Roberta. **Amish Adventure.** Lafayette, CA: C&T Publishing, 1983.

Kiracofe, Roderick and Michael Kile. **The Quilt Digest.** San Francisco, CA: Kiracofe and Kile, 1983.

Lawson, Suzy. **Amish Inspirations.** Cottage Grove, OR: Amity Publications, 1982.

McCauley, Daniel and Kathryn. **Decorative Arts of the Amish of Lancaster County.** Intercourse, PA: Good Books, 1988.

Orlovsky, Patsy and Myron. **Quilts in America.** New York: McGraw Hill Book Company, 1974.

Pellman, Rachel T. and Kenneth. **The World of Amish Quilts.** Intercourse, PA: Good Books, 1984.

_____.**Amish Crib Quilts.** Intercourse, PA: Good Books, 1985.

_____.**Amish Dolls, Doll Quilts, and Other Playthings.** Intercourse, PA, Good Books, 1986.

Pellman, Rachel T. **Amish Quilt Patterns.** Intercourse, PA: Good Books, 1984.

_____.**Small Amish Quilt Patterns.** Intercourse, PA: Good Books, 1985.

Pellman, Rachel T. and Joanne Ranck. **Quilts Among the Plain People.** Intercourse, PA: Good Books, 1981.

Pottinger, David. **Quilts from the Indiana Amish.** New York: E.P. Dutton, Inc., 1983.

Stoltzfus, Louise. **Favorite Recipes from Quilters.** Intercourse, PA: Good Books, 1992.

Tomlonson, Judy Schroeder. **Mennonite Quilts and Pieces.** Intercourse, PA: Good Books, 1985.

About the Mennonites

Bender, Harold S., et al., eds. **The Mennonite Encyclopedia. Vols. I-IV.** Scottdale, Pa.: Herald Press, 1955-1959.

Bender, H.S. **The Anabaptist Vision.** Scottdale, PA: Herald Press, 1967.

Braght, Theileman J. van, comp. **The Bloody Theatre or Martyrs Mirror.** Scottdale, PA: Herald Press, 1951.

Dyck, Cornelius J., ed. **An Introduction to Mennonite History: A Popular History of the Anabaptists and the Mennonites.** Scottdale, PA., and Kitchener, Ont.: Herald Press, 1981.

Dyck, Cornelius J. and Dennis D. Martin, ed. **The Mennonite Encyclopedia: A Comprehensive Reference Work on the Anabaptist-Mennonite Movement. Vol. V:A-Z.** Scottdale, PA.: Herald Press, 1990.

Friesen, Steve. **A Modest Mennonite Home,** Intercourse, PA: Good Books, 1990.

Good, Merle and Phyllis Pellman Good. **20 Most Asked Questions about the Amish and Mennonites.** Intercourse, PA: Good Books, 1979.

Good, Phyllis Pellman. **The Festival Cookbook: Four Seasons of Favorites.** Intercourse, PA: Good Books, 1983.

Good, Phyllis Pellman and Rachel Thomas Pellman. **Amish and Mennonite Kitchens.** Intercourse, PA: Good Books, 1984.

Good, Phyllis Pellman and Louise Stoltzfus. **The Best of Mennonite Fellowship Meals.** Intercourse, PA: Good Books, 1991.

Janzen, Jean, Yorifumi Yaguchi and David Waltner-Toews. **Three Mennonite Poets.** Intercourse, PA: Good Books, 1986.

Janzen, Reinhild Kauenhoven and John M. Janzen. **Mennonite Furniture: A Migrant Tradition (1766-1910).** Intercourse, PA: Good Books, 1991.

Juhnke, James C. **The Mennonite Experience in America, Vol. III. Vision, Doctrine, War: Mennonite Identity and Organization in America 1890-1930.** Scottdale, PA., and Kitchner, Ont.: Herald Press, 1989.

Keim, Albert N. **The CPS Story: An Illustrated History of Civilian Public Service.** Intercourse, PA: Good Books, 1990.

Klaassen, Walter. **Anabaptism: Neither Catholic nor Protestant.** Waterloo, ON: Conrad Press, 1972.

Kraybill, Donald B. **Passing on the Faith.** Intercourse, PA: Good Books, 1991.

Lesher, Emerson L. **The Muppie Manual.** Intercourse, PA: Good Books, 1985.

MacMaster, Richard K. **The Mennonite Experience in America, Vol. I. Land, Piety, Peoplehood: The Establishment of Mennonite Communities in America 1683-1790.** Scottdale, PA., and Kitchener, Ont.: Herald Press, 1988.

Ortiz, Jose and David Graybill. **Reflections of an Hispanic Mennonite.** Intercourse, PA: Good Books, 1989.

Oyer, John S. and Robert S. Kreider. **Mirror of the Martyrs.** Intercourse, PA: Good Books, 1990.

Peachey, Titus and Linda Gehman Peachey. **Seeking Peace.** Intercourse, PA: Good Books, 1991.

Shenk, Sara Wenger. **Coming Home.** Intercourse, PA: Good Books, 1992.

_____. **Why Not Celebrate!** Intercourse, PA: Good Books, 1987.

Schlabach, Theron F. **The Mennonite Experience in America, Vol. II. Peace, Faith, Nation: Mennonites and Amish in Nineteenth-Century America.** Scottdale, PA., and Kitchener, Ont.: Herald Press, 1988.

Voth, Norma Jost. **Mennonite Foods and Folkways from South Russia, Volume I.** Intercourse, PA: Good Books, 1990.

_____. **Mennonite Foods and Folkways from South Russia, Volume II.** Intercourse, PA: Good Books, 1991.

Index

About the Authors

The Pellmans are well-known as the authors of *A Treasury of Amish Quilts, The World of Amish Quilts, Amish Crib Quilts* and *Amish Doll Quilts, Dolls and Other Playthings.*

Rachel Thomas Pellman is manager of The Old Country Store in Intercourse, Pennsylvania, which features quilts, crafts and toys made by more than 350 Amish and Mennonite craftspersons. She is also the curator of The People's Place Quilt Museum in the village of Intercourse. A graduate of Eastern Mennonite College, she has written *Amish Quilt Patterns* and *Small Amish Quilt Patterns.* She has also co-authored *The Country Bride Quilt, The Country Love Quilt, The Country Lily Quilt, The Country Songbird Quilt, The Country Bride Collection, The Country Paradise Quilt, Country Quilts for Children, Favorite Applique Patterns from the Old Country Store—Volume 1, Favorite Applique Patterns from the Old Country Store—Volume 2, Favorite Applique Patterns from the Old Country Store—Volume 3,* and 12 Pennsylvania Dutch Cookbooks.

Kenneth R. Pellman is general manager of The People's Place, an educational center concerned with Amish and Mennonite arts, faith and culture. Kenny graduated from Eastern Mennonite College, where he was also a faculty member in the drama department. His photography has appeared in many books, including a National Geographic publication. He has also co-authored *Living Without Electricity.*

The Pellmans were married in 1976. They live in Lancaster, Pennsylvania, with their two sons, Nathaniel and Jesse. They are members of Rossmere Mennonite Church.

This new book by two well-known experts brings together an extraordinary collection of 149 dazzling quilts from Mennonite communities across North America.

These quilts are monuments of beauty, providing links to earlier generations, serving as precious reminders of long-held values and traditions. Also included are many stories and old photos.

The Pellmans have also authored *A Treasury of Amish Quilts* and many other highly-acclaimed books related to Amish and Mennonite life as well as quilting and collectibles.

51995

$19.95

9 781561 480593

ISBN 1-56148-059-2

THE PEOPLE
YOU MAY SEE

Written and Illustrated by Lisa Koehler